50 Japanese Ramen Noodles Recipes for Home

By: Kelly Johnson

Table of Contents

- Shoyu Ramen
- Miso Ramen
- Shio Ramen
- Tonkotsu Ramen
- Chicken Ramen
- Spicy Tan Tan Men
- Tsukemen (Dipping Noodles)
- Shrimp Ramen
- Vegetarian Ramen
- Sesame Garlic Ramen
- Sapporo Ramen
- Nagoya Ramen
- Hakata Ramen
- Hokkaido Ramen
- Seafood Ramen
- Tokyo Shoyu Ramen
- Lobster Ramen
- Five-Spice Ramen
- Curry Ramen
- Kimchi Ramen
- Cold Ramen (Hiyashi Chuka)
- Green Tea Ramen
- Duck Ramen
- Beef Ramen
- Okinawa Soba
- Clam Ramen
- Cilantro Lime Ramen
- Teriyaki Chicken Ramen
- Shrimp Tempura Ramen
- Garlic Butter Ramen
- Yuzu Ramen
- Sukiyaki Ramen
- Shrimp and Pork Wonton Ramen
- Udon Noodle Soup
- Vegan Ramen

- Truffle Ramen
- Char Siu Ramen
- Egg Drop Ramen
- Lemon Soy Ramen
- Braised Pork Belly Ramen
- Crab Ramen
- Gyoza Ramen
- Green Curry Ramen
- Peanut Sesame Ramen
- Taiwanese Beef Noodle Soup
- Tomato Basil Ramen
- Shrimp and Coconut Ramen
- Chicken Katsu Ramen
- Tantanmen
- Tempura Udon

Shoyu Ramen

Ingredients:

For the Broth:

      8 cups chicken or vegetable broth
      1 onion, halved
      4 cloves garlic, crushed
      2-inch piece of ginger, sliced
      1/2 cup soy sauce
      2 tablespoons mirin
      1 tablespoon sake
      1 tablespoon sesame oil
      1 tablespoon vegetable oil

For the Tare (Seasoning Base):

10. 1/2 cup soy sauce

      2 tablespoons mirin
      1 tablespoon sake

For the Toppings:

13. Ramen noodles

      Chashu pork slices (or substitute with roasted chicken or tofu for a vegetarian option)
      Soft-boiled eggs, halved
      Nori (seaweed) sheets, sliced
      Green onions, finely chopped
      Corn kernels (optional)
      Bamboo shoots (menma)

Instructions:

1. Prepare the Broth:

- In a large pot, heat vegetable oil over medium heat. Add onion, garlic, and ginger. Sauté until fragrant.
- Pour in the chicken or vegetable broth and bring to a simmer. Add soy sauce, mirin, sake, and sesame oil. Let it simmer for at least 30 minutes.

2. Make the Tare:

- In a small saucepan, combine soy sauce, mirin, and sake for the tare. Bring to a simmer and cook for a few minutes until slightly thickened. Set aside.

3. Cook the Toppings:

- Cook the ramen noodles according to package instructions. Prepare soft-boiled eggs, slice nori, chop green onions, and cook any additional toppings you prefer.

4. Assemble the Ramen:

- Strain the broth to remove solid ingredients. Taste and adjust the seasoning if necessary.
- In each serving bowl, add a portion of the tare (seasoning base).
- Pour the hot broth over the tare in each bowl.

5. Add Toppings:

- Arrange cooked ramen noodles in the broth.
- Add chashu pork slices, soft-boiled eggs, nori, green onions, corn, and bamboo shoots.

6. Serve:

- Serve the Shoyu Ramen hot and enjoy the rich, savory flavors.

Tips:

- Customize the toppings to your liking. Popular additions include bean sprouts, mushrooms, or spinach.
- Adjust the soy sauce quantity in the broth and tare to control the saltiness according to your taste.
- Experiment with different types of noodles for a unique texture.

Miso Ramen

Ingredients:

For the broth:

- 4 cups chicken or vegetable broth
- 2 tablespoons miso paste (adjust to taste)
- 1 tablespoon soy sauce
- 1 tablespoon sesame oil
- 1 teaspoon grated ginger
- 2 cloves garlic, minced

For the ramen:

- Ramen noodles (enough for serving)
- Sliced green onions
- Sliced mushrooms (shiitake or other varieties)
- Baby spinach or bok choy
- Sliced carrots
- Soft-boiled eggs (optional)
- Seaweed (nori) sheets, shredded

Instructions:

1. In a pot, heat sesame oil over medium heat. Add minced garlic and grated ginger, sautéing until fragrant.
2. Pour in the chicken or vegetable broth and bring it to a simmer.
3. In a small bowl, mix the miso paste with a ladle of the hot broth until smooth.
4. Add this miso mixture back into the pot, stirring well.
5. Add soy sauce to the broth and let it simmer for about 10-15 minutes, allowing the flavors to meld. Adjust the seasoning to taste.
6. While the broth simmers, cook the ramen noodles according to the package instructions. Drain and set aside.
7. In a separate pan, sauté the mushrooms, carrots, and any other vegetables you choose to include until they are tender.
8. Assemble the ramen bowls by placing a serving of cooked noodles in each bowl. Ladle the hot miso broth over the noodles.

Add the sautéed vegetables, sliced green onions, and any other desired toppings such as soft-boiled eggs or shredded seaweed.
Serve immediately and enjoy your homemade miso ramen!

Feel free to customize the recipe based on your preferences and dietary restrictions. Miso ramen is versatile, allowing you to experiment with different toppings and ingredients.

Shio Ramen

Ingredients:

For the Broth:

- 4-5 cups chicken broth (homemade or store-bought)
- 2-3 cups water
- 2-3 slices of ginger
- 2-3 cloves of garlic, crushed
- Salt, to taste

For the Tare:

- 2 tablespoons soy sauce
- 1 tablespoon mirin (sweet rice wine)
- 1 teaspoon sake
- Salt, to taste

Other Ingredients:

- Ramen noodles (enough for your servings)
- Chashu (sliced, braised or roasted pork belly)
- Ajitsuke Tamago (soft-boiled or marinated eggs)
- Chopped green onions (negi)
- Nori (dried seaweed sheets)
- Optional: Menma (fermented bamboo shoots), spinach, or other toppings of your choice.

Instructions:

1. Prepare the Broth:

In a large pot, combine the chicken broth, water, ginger, and garlic.
Bring the mixture to a simmer over medium heat.
Let it simmer for at least 30 minutes to allow the flavors to meld.
Season the broth with salt to taste. Keep in mind that the tare will also add some saltiness, so start with a small amount and adjust as needed.

2. Make the Tare:

In a small bowl, mix together the soy sauce, mirin, sake, and salt.
Adjust the seasoning to your taste preferences.

3. Prepare Toppings:

> Cook the ramen noodles according to the package instructions. Drain and set aside.
> Slice the chashu into thin pieces.
> Prepare the ajitsuke tamago (soft-boiled or marinated eggs).
> Chop green onions and any other toppings you plan to use.

4. Assemble the Shio Ramen:

> Place a portion of cooked ramen noodles in each serving bowl.
> Pour the hot broth over the noodles.
> Add a spoonful or two of the tare to each bowl, adjusting based on your desired saltiness.
> Arrange the chashu, ajitsuke tamago, chopped green onions, nori, and any additional toppings over the noodles.
> Serve immediately and enjoy your homemade shio ramen!

Feel free to experiment with the recipe to suit your taste. You can also add or omit ingredients based on your preferences. Enjoy your delicious bowl of shio ramen!

Tonkotsu Ramen

Ingredients:

For the Broth:

- 4-5 pounds pork bones (knuckle and trotter bones work well)
- 1 onion, halved
- 1 leek, roughly chopped
- 4 cloves garlic, crushed
- 1 knob ginger, sliced
- 2 tablespoons vegetable oil
- Water (enough to cover the bones)
- Salt, to taste

For the Tare (Seasoning):

- 1/2 cup soy sauce
- 1/4 cup sake
- 1/4 cup mirin
- 1 tablespoon sugar

Other Ingredients:

- Ramen noodles (enough for your servings)
- Chashu (sliced, braised or roasted pork belly)
- Ajitsuke Tamago (soft-boiled or marinated eggs)
- Green onions, chopped
- Nori (dried seaweed sheets)
- Optional: Menma (fermented bamboo shoots), corn, or other desired toppings.

Instructions:

1. Prepare the Broth:

    Blanch the Bones:
    - Rinse the pork bones under cold water.
    - Bring a large pot of water to boil and add the bones. Boil vigorously for 10-15 minutes to remove impurities.
    - Discard the water and rinse the bones again.

    Cook the Broth:

- In a large, clean pot, heat vegetable oil over medium-high heat.
- Add onion, leek, garlic, and ginger. Sauté until aromatic.
- Add the blanched pork bones to the pot.
- Cover the bones with water and bring to a boil.
- Reduce heat to a low simmer and cook for at least 6-8 hours, skimming off any impurities that rise to the surface.
- Add salt to taste during the last hour of cooking.

Strain the Broth:
- Strain the broth through a fine mesh strainer or cheesecloth to remove bones and solids.
- Your tonkotsu broth is ready.

2. Make the Tare:

In a small saucepan, combine soy sauce, sake, mirin, and sugar.
Simmer over low heat until the sugar dissolves. Set aside to cool.

3. Prepare Toppings:

Cook the ramen noodles according to the package instructions. Drain and set aside.
Slice the chashu into thin pieces.
Prepare the ajitsuke tamago (soft-boiled or marinated eggs).
Chop green onions and any other desired toppings.

4. Assemble the Tonkotsu Ramen:

Place a portion of cooked ramen noodles in each serving bowl.
Pour the hot tonkotsu broth over the noodles.
Add a spoonful of the tare to each bowl, adjusting based on your taste.
Arrange the chashu, ajitsuke tamago, chopped green onions, nori, and any additional toppings over the noodles.
Serve immediately and enjoy your homemade Tonkotsu Ramen!

Remember, making Tonkotsu Ramen requires patience, but the result is a flavorful and satisfying bowl of ramen. Feel free to customize the recipe to your liking!

Chicken Ramen

Ingredients:

For the Broth:

- 1 whole chicken (about 3-4 pounds), cut into pieces
- 1 onion, quartered
- 3 carrots, chopped
- 4 cloves garlic, smashed
- 1 knob ginger, sliced
- 2 stalks celery, chopped
- 8 cups chicken broth (homemade or store-bought)
- 2 tablespoons soy sauce
- 1 tablespoon mirin (optional)
- Salt and pepper, to taste

For the Tare (Seasoning):

- 3 tablespoons soy sauce
- 1 tablespoon mirin
- 1 teaspoon sesame oil (optional)

Other Ingredients:

- Ramen noodles (enough for your servings)
- Chopped green onions
- Sliced mushrooms
- Bok choy or spinach, blanched
- Soft-boiled eggs (ajitsuke tamago)
- Nori (dried seaweed sheets), sliced

Instructions:

1. Prepare the Broth:

> In a large pot, combine the chicken pieces, onion, carrots, garlic, ginger, celery, and chicken broth.
> Bring the mixture to a boil and then reduce the heat to a simmer.
> Simmer for about 1 to 1.5 hours, skimming off any impurities that rise to the surface.

Once the chicken is fully cooked and the flavors have infused into the broth, remove the chicken pieces and shred the meat. Discard the bones and skin.

2. Make the Tare:

In a small bowl, mix together soy sauce, mirin, and sesame oil (if using).

3. Assemble the Chicken Ramen:

Cook the ramen noodles according to the package instructions. Drain and set aside.
Adjust the seasoning of the broth with soy sauce, mirin (if using), salt, and pepper to taste.
Place a portion of cooked ramen noodles in each serving bowl.
Pour the hot chicken broth over the noodles.
Add a spoonful of the tare to each bowl, adjusting based on your taste.
Arrange shredded chicken, chopped green onions, sliced mushrooms, blanched bok choy or spinach, and soft-boiled eggs over the noodles.
Garnish with sliced nori.

Serve immediately and enjoy your homemade chicken ramen!

Feel free to customize the toppings and adjust the seasonings to suit your preferences. Chicken ramen offers a lighter and equally flavorful option compared to other ramen varieties.

Spicy Tan Tan Men

Ingredients:

For the Broth:

- 1 tablespoon sesame oil
- 2 tablespoons miso paste (white or red)
- 2 tablespoons tahini (sesame paste)
- 1 tablespoon soy sauce
- 1 tablespoon chili oil (adjust to taste for desired spice level)
- 1 tablespoon grated ginger
- 2 cloves garlic, minced
- 4 cups vegetable or chicken broth
- 1 cup water
- Salt and pepper, to taste

For the Topping:

- 1/2 pound ground pork or chicken
- 2 tablespoons soy sauce
- 1 tablespoon mirin
- 1 tablespoon sake
- 1 teaspoon sugar
- 2 green onions, chopped
- 1 cup bean sprouts
- Cooked ramen noodles (enough for your servings)

Optional Garnishes:

- Crushed peanuts
- Sesame seeds
- Chili flakes
- Sliced green onions

Instructions:

For the Broth:

In a large pot, heat sesame oil over medium heat. Add grated ginger and minced garlic, sauté for 1-2 minutes until fragrant.
Add miso paste, tahini, soy sauce, and chili oil to the pot. Stir well to combine.

Pour in the vegetable or chicken broth and water. Bring the mixture to a simmer. Season with salt and pepper to taste. Allow the broth to simmer for about 15-20 minutes, allowing the flavors to meld.

For the Topping:

In a separate pan, cook the ground pork or chicken over medium heat until browned.
Add soy sauce, mirin, sake, and sugar to the meat. Cook for an additional 2-3 minutes until the sauce thickens.
Add chopped green onions and bean sprouts to the pan. Cook for another 1-2 minutes until the vegetables are slightly tender.

Assembling Spicy Tan Tan Men:

Cook the ramen noodles according to the package instructions. Drain and set aside.
Ladle the spicy sesame broth into serving bowls.
Place a portion of cooked ramen noodles in each bowl.
Spoon the ground pork or chicken mixture over the noodles.
Garnish with crushed peanuts, sesame seeds, chili flakes, and additional sliced green onions, if desired.

Serve immediately, and enjoy your delicious and spicy Tan Tan Men! Adjust the spice level and toppings according to your preferences.

Tsukemen (Dipping Noodles)

Ingredients:

For the Noodles:

- Fresh or dried ramen noodles

For the Dipping Sauce (Tare):

- Soy sauce
- Mirin (sweet rice wine)
- Sake (Japanese rice wine)
- Dashi (Japanese soup stock)
- Sugar
- Garlic (minced)
- Ginger (grated)

Toppings (Optional):

- Sliced green onions
- Nori (seaweed)
- Menma (fermented bamboo shoots)
- Chashu (braised pork slices)
- Soft-boiled egg (halved)

Instructions:

Prepare the Noodles:
- Cook the ramen noodles according to the package instructions.
- Once cooked, drain and rinse the noodles under cold running water to stop the cooking process.

Make the Dipping Sauce (Tare):
- In a saucepan, combine soy sauce, mirin, sake, dashi, sugar, minced garlic, and grated ginger.
- Bring the mixture to a simmer over medium heat, stirring to dissolve the sugar.
- Simmer for a few minutes until the flavors meld. Adjust the sweetness or saltiness according to your taste.
- Allow the dipping sauce to cool before serving.

Prepare Toppings:

- Slice green onions, prepare nori, menma, chashu, and soft-boiled eggs as desired.

Serve:
- Place the cooled noodles on a plate or in a separate bowl.
- Pour the dipping sauce into individual serving bowls.

Dip and Enjoy:
- Take a small portion of noodles with your chopsticks and dip them into the sauce.
- Garnish with your preferred toppings.
- Enjoy the flavorful combination of chewy noodles and the concentrated dipping sauce.

Tsukemen provides a unique and satisfying dining experience, allowing you to control the noodle-to-broth ratio and savor the rich flavors of the dipping sauce. Feel free to customize the dish with your favorite toppings and adjust the sauce ingredients to suit your taste preferences.

Shrimp Ramen

Ingredients:

For the Broth:

- 4 cups chicken or vegetable broth
- 1 cup shrimp stock (can be made by simmering shrimp shells in water)
- 2 cloves garlic, minced
- 1 tablespoon ginger, grated
- 2 tablespoons soy sauce
- 1 tablespoon mirin (optional)
- 1 tablespoon sesame oil
- Salt and pepper to taste

For the Ramen:

- Ramen noodles (enough for the number of servings)
- Shrimp, peeled and deveined
- Vegetables (bok choy, spinach, mushrooms, and green onions work well)
- Hard-boiled eggs, halved (optional)
- Nori (seaweed), sliced (optional)
- Sesame seeds for garnish (optional)

Instructions:

Prepare the Broth:
- In a pot, combine the chicken or vegetable broth and shrimp stock.
- Add minced garlic, grated ginger, soy sauce, mirin (if using), sesame oil, salt, and pepper.
- Bring the broth to a simmer over medium heat and let it cook for about 15-20 minutes to allow the flavors to meld.

Cook the Shrimp:
- Season the shrimp with salt and pepper.
- In a separate pan, heat a bit of oil over medium-high heat.
- Add the shrimp and cook until they turn pink and opaque. Remove from heat and set aside.

Prepare the Vegetables:
- Sauté or blanch your choice of vegetables (bok choy, spinach, mushrooms) until they are tender-crisp.

Cook the Ramen Noodles:
- Cook the ramen noodles according to the package instructions. Drain and set aside.

Assemble the Shrimp Ramen:
- Divide the cooked noodles among serving bowls.
- Pour the hot broth over the noodles.
- Arrange the cooked shrimp, vegetables, and any optional toppings (hard-boiled eggs, nori, sesame seeds) on top.

Serve:
- Serve the shrimp ramen hot and enjoy!

Feel free to customize the recipe by adding other ingredients like corn, bean sprouts, or tofu. Adjust the seasoning to your liking, and you'll have a delicious bowl of homemade shrimp ramen.

Vegetarian Ramen

Ingredients:

For the Broth:

- 6 cups vegetable broth
- 1 onion, sliced
- 4 cloves garlic, minced
- 1 tablespoon fresh ginger, grated
- 2 tablespoons soy sauce
- 1 tablespoon miso paste
- 1 tablespoon sesame oil
- 1 tablespoon mirin (optional)
- Salt and pepper to taste

For the Ramen:

- Ramen noodles (enough for the number of servings)
- Tofu, cubed and pan-fried
- Assorted vegetables (bok choy, mushrooms, carrots, spinach, green onions, corn, bean sprouts, etc.)
- Nori (seaweed), sliced
- Sesame seeds for garnish
- Chili oil or hot sauce (optional)

Instructions:

Prepare the Broth:
- In a pot, sauté the sliced onion, minced garlic, and grated ginger in sesame oil until softened.
- Add vegetable broth, soy sauce, miso paste, mirin (if using), salt, and pepper.
- Bring the broth to a simmer and let it cook for about 15-20 minutes to develop flavors.

Cook the Ramen Noodles:
- Cook the ramen noodles according to the package instructions. Drain and set aside.

Prepare Tofu and Vegetables:
- Cube the tofu and pan-fry until golden brown on all sides.

- Sauté or blanch a variety of vegetables such as bok choy, mushrooms, carrots, spinach, green onions, corn, or bean sprouts.

Assemble the Vegetarian Ramen:
- Divide the cooked noodles among serving bowls.
- Pour the hot broth over the noodles.
- Arrange the cooked tofu, assorted vegetables, and any additional toppings like nori, sesame seeds, or chili oil on top.

Serve:
- Serve the vegetarian ramen hot, and enjoy the delightful flavors of the plant-based ingredients.

Feel free to customize your vegetarian ramen by adding other favorite vegetables or plant-based protein sources. Adjust the seasoning to your taste, and you'll have a comforting and wholesome bowl of vegetarian ramen.

Sesame Garlic Ramen

Ingredients:

For the Broth:

- 4 cups vegetable or mushroom broth
- 4 cloves garlic, minced
- 2 tablespoons soy sauce
- 1 tablespoon sesame oil
- 1 tablespoon rice vinegar
- 1 tablespoon mirin (optional)
- 1 tablespoon hoisin sauce
- Salt and pepper to taste

For the Ramen:

- Ramen noodles (enough for the number of servings)
- 1 tablespoon sesame oil (for cooking noodles)
- Vegetables (bok choy, sliced mushrooms, shredded carrots, spinach, etc.)
- Green onions, chopped, for garnish
- Sesame seeds for garnish
- Red pepper flakes (optional for spice)

Instructions:

Prepare the Broth:
- In a pot, sauté the minced garlic in sesame oil until fragrant.
- Add vegetable or mushroom broth, soy sauce, rice vinegar, mirin (if using), hoisin sauce, salt, and pepper.
- Bring the broth to a simmer and let it cook for about 10-15 minutes to infuse the flavors.

Cook the Ramen Noodles:
- Cook the ramen noodles according to the package instructions. Drain and toss with a tablespoon of sesame oil to prevent sticking.

Prepare Vegetables:
- Sauté or blanch your choice of vegetables (bok choy, mushrooms, shredded carrots, spinach) until they are tender-crisp.

Assemble the Sesame Garlic Ramen:
- Divide the cooked noodles among serving bowls.
- Pour the hot broth over the noodles.

- Arrange the cooked vegetables on top.

Garnish and Serve:
- Garnish with chopped green onions, sesame seeds, and red pepper flakes for some spice if desired.

Optional Additions:
- You can add protein sources like tofu, edamame, or a soft-boiled egg for extra texture and flavor.

Serve:
- Serve the Sesame Garlic Ramen hot and enjoy the rich, nutty, and garlicky flavors.

Feel free to adjust the ingredients and quantities based on your taste preferences. This Sesame Garlic Ramen is a comforting and flavorful dish that's easy to make at home.

Sapporo Ramen

Ingredients:

For the Broth:

- 6 cups chicken or vegetable broth
- 1 onion, sliced
- 4 cloves garlic, minced
- 2 tablespoons ginger, grated
- 3 tablespoons miso paste (preferably red or brown miso)
- 2 tablespoons soy sauce
- 1 tablespoon mirin
- 1 tablespoon sesame oil
- Salt and pepper to taste

For the Ramen:

- Sapporo-style ramen noodles (these are typically thicker and wavy)
- Chashu pork slices or pork belly, thinly sliced
- Corn kernels (canned or frozen)
- Bean sprouts
- Green onions, chopped
- Nori (seaweed), sliced
- Menma (fermented bamboo shoots)
- Butter (optional)

Instructions:

Prepare the Broth:
- In a pot, sauté the sliced onion, minced garlic, and grated ginger in sesame oil until softened.
- Add chicken or vegetable broth, miso paste, soy sauce, mirin, salt, and pepper.
- Bring the broth to a simmer and let it cook for about 15-20 minutes to develop flavors.

Prepare Toppings:
- Cook the Sapporo-style ramen noodles according to the package instructions.
- Cook chashu pork slices or pork belly until fully cooked and thinly slice.

- Prepare corn kernels, bean sprouts, chopped green onions, sliced nori, and menma.

Assemble the Sapporo Ramen:
- Divide the cooked noodles among serving bowls.
- Pour the hot miso broth over the noodles.

Add Toppings:
- Arrange slices of chashu pork, corn kernels, bean sprouts, green onions, nori, and menma on top of the noodles.

Optional Butter Finish:
- For a classic Sapporo Ramen touch, add a small pat of butter to the hot broth and let it melt.

Serve:
- Serve the Sapporo Ramen hot and enjoy the rich and hearty flavors.

Feel free to customize the toppings and adjust the seasoning to suit your preferences.

Sapporo Ramen is a hearty and flavorful dish that combines the umami of miso with a variety of delicious toppings.

Nagoya Ramen

Ingredients:

For the Broth:

- 6 cups chicken or pork broth
- 1 onion, sliced
- 4 cloves garlic, minced
- 2 tablespoons ginger, grated
- 3 tablespoons red miso paste
- 2 tablespoons soy sauce
- 1 tablespoon sake
- 1 tablespoon mirin
- 1 tablespoon sesame oil
- Salt and pepper to taste

For the Ramen:

- Ramen noodles (enough for the number of servings)
- Chashu pork slices or pork belly, thinly sliced
- Green onions, chopped
- Kikurage mushrooms (wood ear mushrooms), rehydrated and sliced
- Naruto (fish cake), sliced
- Menma (fermented bamboo shoots)
- Red pickled ginger (beni shoga)
- Ajitsuke Tamago (marinated soft-boiled egg)

Instructions:

Prepare the Broth:
- In a pot, sauté the sliced onion, minced garlic, and grated ginger in sesame oil until softened.
- Add chicken or pork broth, red miso paste, soy sauce, sake, mirin, salt, and pepper.
- Bring the broth to a simmer and let it cook for about 15-20 minutes to develop flavors.

Prepare Toppings:
- Cook the ramen noodles according to the package instructions.
- Cook chashu pork slices or pork belly until fully cooked and thinly slice.

- Rehydrate kikurage mushrooms and slice them.
- Slice naruto (fish cake), prepare menma, and have red pickled ginger ready.
- Prepare Ajitsuke Tamago (marinated soft-boiled egg).

Assemble the Nagoya Ramen:
- Divide the cooked noodles among serving bowls.
- Pour the hot red miso broth over the noodles.

Add Toppings:
- Arrange slices of chashu pork, green onions, kikurage mushrooms, naruto, menma, and red pickled ginger on top of the noodles.

Place Ajitsuke Tamago:
- Slice the marinated soft-boiled eggs in half and place them in the bowl.

Serve:
- Serve the Nagoya Ramen hot and enjoy the robust flavors of the red miso broth and the various toppings.

Feel free to customize the toppings and adjust the seasoning to your liking. Nagoya Ramen offers a unique and flavorful experience, with the rich miso broth being the star of the dish.

Hakata Ramen

Ingredients:

For the Broth:

- 8 cups water
- 2–3 pounds pork trotters or pork bones (split)
- 1 onion, halved
- 1 leek, cut into large pieces
- 1 piece ginger (about 2 inches), sliced
- 4 cloves garlic, smashed
- 2 dried shiitake mushrooms (optional)
- 1 tablespoon vegetable oil
- Salt to taste

For the Tare (Flavor Concentrate):

- 1/2 cup soy sauce
- 1/4 cup sake
- 2 tablespoons mirin

For the Ramen:

- Hakata-style ramen noodles
- Chashu pork slices or pork belly, thinly sliced
- Green onions, chopped
- Beni shoga (red pickled ginger)
- Kikurage mushrooms (wood ear mushrooms), rehydrated and sliced
- Ajitsuke Tamago (marinated soft-boiled eggs)

Instructions:

Prepare the Broth:
- Clean pork bones thoroughly and soak them in water for a few hours to remove excess blood.
- In a large pot, bring water to a boil. Add pork bones, onion, leek, ginger, garlic, and shiitake mushrooms. Boil vigorously for 10 minutes, then discard the water.
- Rinse the bones and pot. Add fresh water and return the bones to the pot.

- Simmer the bones on low heat for 8-12 hours, periodically skimming off any impurities that rise to the surface.
- Strain the broth through a fine-mesh strainer. Season with salt to taste.

Prepare the Tare:
- In a small saucepan, combine soy sauce, sake, and mirin. Simmer over low heat for about 5 minutes. Set aside.

Prepare Toppings:
- Cook the Hakata-style ramen noodles according to the package instructions.
- Cook chashu pork slices or pork belly until fully cooked and thinly slice.
- Rehydrate kikurage mushrooms and slice them.
- Prepare green onions and beni shoga.

Assemble the Hakata Ramen:
- Divide the cooked noodles among serving bowls.
- Pour the hot tonkotsu broth over the noodles.
- Add a spoonful of tare (flavor concentrate) to each bowl.

Add Toppings:
- Arrange slices of chashu pork, kikurage mushrooms, green onions, and beni shoga on top of the noodles.

Place Ajitsuke Tamago:
- Slice the marinated soft-boiled eggs in half and place them in the bowl.

Serve:
- Serve the Hakata Ramen hot and enjoy the rich, creamy tonkotsu broth and the various toppings.

Hakata Ramen is known for its intense pork flavor and simple yet satisfying toppings. Adjust the salt and tare levels to your preference, and you'll have an authentic bowl of Hakata-style ramen at home.

Hokkaido Ramen

Ingredients:

For the Broth:

- 6 cups chicken or vegetable broth
- 1 onion, sliced
- 4 cloves garlic, minced
- 2 tablespoons ginger, grated
- 3 tablespoons miso paste (white or red miso)
- 2 tablespoons soy sauce
- 1 tablespoon mirin
- 1 tablespoon sake
- 1 tablespoon sesame oil
- Salt and pepper to taste

For the Ramen:

- Ramen noodles (enough for the number of servings)
- Chashu pork slices or pork belly, thinly sliced
- Corn kernels (canned or frozen)
- Butter (about 1 tablespoon per serving)
- Green onions, chopped
- Nori (seaweed), sliced
- Menma (fermented bamboo shoots)
- Ajitsuke Tamago (marinated soft-boiled egg)

Instructions:

Prepare the Broth:
- In a pot, sauté the sliced onion, minced garlic, and grated ginger in sesame oil until softened.
- Add chicken or vegetable broth, miso paste, soy sauce, mirin, sake, salt, and pepper.
- Bring the broth to a simmer and let it cook for about 15-20 minutes to develop flavors.

Prepare Toppings:
- Cook the ramen noodles according to the package instructions.
- Cook chashu pork slices or pork belly until fully cooked and thinly slice.
- Prepare corn kernels (canned or thawed if frozen).

- Slice green onions, nori, and have menma ready.
- Prepare Ajitsuke Tamago (marinated soft-boiled egg).

Assemble the Hokkaido Ramen:
- Divide the cooked noodles among serving bowls.
- Pour the hot miso broth over the noodles.

Add Toppings:
- Add slices of chashu pork, corn kernels, a pat of butter, green onions, nori, and menma to each bowl.

Place Ajitsuke Tamago:
- Slice the marinated soft-boiled eggs in half and place them in the bowl.

Serve:
- Serve the Hokkaido Ramen hot and enjoy the rich miso broth, the creamy butter, and the delightful combination of toppings.

Feel free to adjust the ingredients and quantities based on your taste preferences.

Hokkaido Ramen is known for its hearty and comforting flavors, and the addition of butter and corn adds a unique touch to this regional style of ramen.

Seafood Ramen

Ingredients:

For the Seafood Broth:

- 6 cups seafood stock (you can use a combination of fish stock, clam juice, and/or shrimp stock)
- 1 onion, sliced
- 4 cloves garlic, minced
- 1 tablespoon ginger, grated
- 2 tablespoons soy sauce
- 1 tablespoon mirin
- 1 tablespoon sesame oil
- Salt and pepper to taste

For the Ramen:

- Ramen noodles (enough for the number of servings)
- Assorted seafood (shrimp, squid, mussels, clams, etc.)
- Bok choy, chopped
- Shiitake mushrooms, sliced
- Green onions, chopped
- Nori (seaweed), sliced
- Sesame seeds for garnish
- Red pepper flakes (optional for spice)

Instructions:

Prepare the Seafood Broth:
- In a pot, sauté the sliced onion, minced garlic, and grated ginger in sesame oil until softened.
- Add seafood stock, soy sauce, mirin, salt, and pepper.
- Bring the broth to a simmer and let it cook for about 15-20 minutes to develop flavors.

Prepare Toppings:
- Cook the ramen noodles according to the package instructions.
- Clean and prepare the assorted seafood (shrimp, squid, mussels, clams).
- Sauté or blanch bok choy and shiitake mushrooms until they are tender.

Cook the Seafood:

- Add the assorted seafood to the simmering broth and cook until they are just cooked through. Be careful not to overcook the seafood, as it can become tough.

Assemble the Seafood Ramen:
- Divide the cooked noodles among serving bowls.
- Pour the hot seafood broth over the noodles.

Add Toppings:
- Arrange the cooked seafood, bok choy, shiitake mushrooms, green onions, nori, and sesame seeds on top of the noodles.

Optional Spice:
- If you like some spice, add red pepper flakes to taste.

Serve:
- Serve the seafood ramen hot and enjoy the savory and briny flavors of the seafood broth.

Feel free to customize the recipe with your favorite seafood choices and additional vegetables. Seafood ramen is a light and refreshing option that brings the taste of the ocean to your bowl of noodles.

Tokyo Shoyu Ramen

Ingredients:

For the Shoyu Broth:

- 6 cups chicken or vegetable broth
- 2 tablespoons soy sauce
- 1 tablespoon mirin
- 1 tablespoon sake
- 1 tablespoon sesame oil
- 2 cloves garlic, minced
- 1 teaspoon ginger, grated
- Salt and white pepper to taste

For the Ramen:

- Ramen noodles (enough for the number of servings)
- Chashu pork slices or pork belly, thinly sliced
- Menma (fermented bamboo shoots)
- Naruto (fish cake), sliced
- Green onions, chopped
- Nori (seaweed), sliced
- Ajitsuke Tamago (marinated soft-boiled egg)

Instructions:

Prepare the Shoyu Broth:
- In a pot, sauté the minced garlic and grated ginger in sesame oil until fragrant.
- Add chicken or vegetable broth, soy sauce, mirin, sake, salt, and white pepper.
- Bring the broth to a simmer and let it cook for about 15-20 minutes to develop flavors.

Prepare Toppings:
- Cook the ramen noodles according to the package instructions.
- Cook chashu pork slices or pork belly until fully cooked and thinly slice.
- Slice menma and naruto (fish cake).
- Chop green onions and slice nori. Prepare Ajitsuke Tamago (marinated soft-boiled egg).

Assemble the Tokyo Shoyu Ramen:

- Divide the cooked noodles among serving bowls.
- Pour the hot shoyu broth over the noodles.

Add Toppings:
- Arrange slices of chashu pork, menma, naruto, green onions, nori, and Ajitsuke Tamago on top of the noodles.

Serve:
- Serve the Tokyo Shoyu Ramen hot and enjoy the clean and savory flavors of the soy sauce-based broth.

Feel free to adjust the ingredients and quantities based on your taste preferences. Tokyo Shoyu Ramen is known for its simplicity, allowing the rich and salty notes of the soy sauce to shine through. Enjoy the classic combination of toppings for an authentic Tokyo ramen experience.

Lobster Ramen

Ingredients:

For the Lobster Broth:

- 2 lobster bodies and shells (from 2 large lobsters)
- 2 tablespoons vegetable oil
- 1 onion, chopped
- 2 carrots, chopped
- 2 celery stalks, chopped
- 3 cloves garlic, minced
- 1 tablespoon tomato paste
- 1 cup dry white wine
- 8 cups water
- 1 bay leaf
- 1 teaspoon thyme
- Salt and black pepper to taste

For the Ramen:

- Ramen noodles (enough for the number of servings)
- Lobster meat, cooked and chopped
- Baby bok choy, halved
- Shiitake mushrooms, sliced
- Green onions, chopped
- Nori (seaweed), sliced
- Sesame seeds for garnish
- Lime wedges for serving

Instructions:

Prepare the Lobster Broth:
- In a large pot, heat vegetable oil over medium heat. Add onion, carrots, celery, and garlic. Sauté until vegetables are softened.
- Add lobster bodies and shells. Cook for a few minutes until they turn red.
- Stir in tomato paste and cook for an additional 2 minutes.
- Pour in white wine to deglaze the pot, scraping up any browned bits from the bottom.
- Add water, bay leaf, thyme, salt, and black pepper. Bring to a simmer and let it cook for about 30-45 minutes to extract flavors.

- Strain the broth through a fine-mesh strainer, pressing down on solids to extract all the liquid.

Prepare Toppings:
- Cook the ramen noodles according to the package instructions.
- Cook lobster meat separately, either by boiling, steaming, or grilling. Chop the lobster meat into bite-sized pieces.
- Blanch baby bok choy in hot water until tender-crisp.
- Sauté shiitake mushrooms until they are cooked through.
- Chop green onions and slice nori.

Assemble the Lobster Ramen:
- Divide the cooked noodles among serving bowls.
- Pour the hot lobster broth over the noodles.

Add Toppings:
- Arrange lobster meat, baby bok choy, sautéed shiitake mushrooms, green onions, and nori on top of the noodles.

Garnish and Serve:
- Garnish with sesame seeds and serve with lime wedges on the side.

Lobster ramen is a decadent dish that combines the delicate sweetness of lobster with the umami-rich broth, creating a luxurious and memorable dining experience. Adjust the ingredients and toppings based on your preferences for a personalized touch.

Five-Spice Ramen

Ingredients:

For the Broth:

- 6 cups chicken or vegetable broth
- 1 onion, sliced
- 4 cloves garlic, minced
- 2 tablespoons ginger, grated
- 2 tablespoons soy sauce
- 1 tablespoon mirin
- 1 tablespoon sesame oil
- 1 tablespoon Chinese five-spice powder
- 1 tablespoon miso paste (white or red miso)
- Salt and pepper to taste

For the Ramen:

- Ramen noodles (enough for the number of servings)
- Protein of choice (sliced chicken, pork, tofu, or shrimp)
- Bok choy, chopped
- Shiitake mushrooms, sliced
- Green onions, chopped
- Soft-boiled eggs, halved (optional)
- Sesame seeds for garnish
- Red pepper flakes (optional for spice)

Instructions:

Prepare the Broth:
- In a pot, sauté the sliced onion, minced garlic, and grated ginger in sesame oil until softened.
- Add chicken or vegetable broth, soy sauce, mirin, Chinese five-spice powder, miso paste, salt, and pepper.
- Bring the broth to a simmer and let it cook for about 15-20 minutes to develop flavors.

Prepare Toppings:
- Cook the ramen noodles according to the package instructions.
- Cook the protein of choice (sliced chicken, pork, tofu, or shrimp) and set aside.

- Sauté bok choy and shiitake mushrooms until they are tender-crisp.

Assemble the Five-Spice Ramen:
- Divide the cooked noodles among serving bowls.
- Pour the hot five-spice broth over the noodles.

Add Toppings:
- Arrange the cooked protein, bok choy, shiitake mushrooms, green onions, and soft-boiled eggs (if using) on top of the noodles.

Garnish and Serve:
- Garnish with sesame seeds and, if desired, red pepper flakes for some spice.

Five-Spice Ramen offers a unique and aromatic twist to the traditional ramen experience. Adjust the spice level and toppings based on your preference for a customized and flavorful bowl of ramen.

Curry Ramen

Ingredients:

For the Curry Broth:

- 6 cups vegetable or chicken broth
- 2 tablespoons curry powder
- 1 tablespoon soy sauce
- 1 tablespoon mirin
- 1 tablespoon sesame oil
- 1 onion, finely chopped
- 2 cloves garlic, minced
- 1 tablespoon ginger, grated
- 1 carrot, julienned
- 1 potato, diced
- 1 cup coconut milk (optional, for creaminess)
- Salt and pepper to taste

For the Ramen:

- Ramen noodles (enough for the number of servings)
- Protein of choice (sliced chicken, pork, tofu, or shrimp)
- Vegetables (bok choy, spinach, bell peppers, etc.)
- Green onions, chopped
- Soft-boiled eggs, halved (optional)
- Sesame seeds for garnish

Instructions:

Prepare the Curry Broth:
- In a pot, sauté the chopped onion, minced garlic, and grated ginger in sesame oil until softened.
- Add curry powder and continue sautéing for 1-2 minutes until fragrant.
- Pour in vegetable or chicken broth, soy sauce, mirin, and bring to a simmer.
- Add julienned carrots and diced potatoes. Simmer until the vegetables are tender.
- If desired, add coconut milk for extra creaminess. Season with salt and pepper to taste.

Prepare Toppings:

- Cook the ramen noodles according to the package instructions.
- Cook the protein of choice (sliced chicken, pork, tofu, or shrimp) and set aside.
- Sauté or blanch vegetables like bok choy, spinach, or bell peppers until tender.

Assemble the Curry Ramen:
- Divide the cooked noodles among serving bowls.
- Pour the hot curry broth over the noodles.

Add Toppings:
- Arrange the cooked protein, sautéed or blanched vegetables, green onions, and soft-boiled eggs (if using) on top of the noodles.

Garnish and Serve:
- Garnish with sesame seeds for added texture and flavor.

Curry ramen offers a unique blend of savory and aromatic curry flavors with the comfort of ramen noodles. Adjust the spice level and ingredients to suit your taste preferences and enjoy this delicious fusion dish.

Kimchi Ramen

Ingredients:

For the Kimchi Broth:

- 6 cups vegetable or chicken broth
- 1 cup kimchi, chopped
- 3 tablespoons kimchi juice
- 2 tablespoons soy sauce
- 1 tablespoon sesame oil
- 1 tablespoon gochugaru (Korean red pepper flakes)
- 1 tablespoon miso paste
- 1 onion, sliced
- 4 cloves garlic, minced
- 1 tablespoon ginger, grated
- 1 tablespoon mirin (optional)
- Salt and pepper to taste

For the Ramen:

- Ramen noodles (enough for the number of servings)
- Protein of choice (sliced chicken, pork, tofu, or shrimp)
- Vegetables (bok choy, mushrooms, green onions, etc.)
- Soft-boiled eggs, halved (optional)
- Sesame seeds for garnish
- Nori (seaweed) for garnish
- Toasted sesame oil for drizzling

Instructions:

Prepare the Kimchi Broth:
- In a pot, sauté the sliced onion, minced garlic, and grated ginger in sesame oil until softened.
- Add vegetable or chicken broth, chopped kimchi, kimchi juice, soy sauce, gochugaru, miso paste, mirin, salt, and pepper.
- Bring the broth to a simmer and let it cook for about 15-20 minutes to develop flavors.

Prepare Toppings:
- Cook the ramen noodles according to the package instructions.

- Cook the protein of choice (sliced chicken, pork, tofu, or shrimp) and set aside.
- Sauté or blanch vegetables like bok choy, mushrooms, and green onions until tender.

Assemble the Kimchi Ramen:
- Divide the cooked noodles among serving bowls.
- Pour the hot kimchi broth over the noodles.

Add Toppings:
- Arrange the cooked protein, sautéed or blanched vegetables, and soft-boiled eggs (if using) on top of the noodles.

Garnish and Serve:
- Garnish with sesame seeds, nori, and a drizzle of toasted sesame oil.

Kimchi ramen provides a spicy and umami-packed flavor profile, combining the heat of kimchi with the richness of the broth. Adjust the spice level and toppings to your liking for a personalized bowl of delicious Kimchi Ramen.

Cold Ramen (Hiyashi Chuka)

Ingredients:

For the Sauce:

- 3 tablespoons soy sauce
- 2 tablespoons rice vinegar
- 1 tablespoon sesame oil
- 1 tablespoon mirin
- 1 tablespoon sugar
- 1 teaspoon grated ginger
- 1 teaspoon grated garlic

For the Cold Ramen:

- Chilled ramen noodles (enough for the number of servings)
- Thinly sliced ham or roast pork
- Cucumber, julienned
- Carrot, julienned or shredded
- Red bell pepper, thinly sliced
- Bean sprouts
- Nori (seaweed), sliced into thin strips
- Chopped green onions
- Sesame seeds for garnish
- Optional toppings: shredded omelet, shrimp, or any other preferred ingredients

Instructions:

Prepare the Sauce:
- In a small bowl, whisk together soy sauce, rice vinegar, sesame oil, mirin, sugar, grated ginger, and grated garlic. Adjust the taste according to your preference.

Prepare Toppings:
- Cook and chill the ramen noodles according to the package instructions. Rinse them under cold water to stop the cooking process, and then chill them in the refrigerator.
- Prepare the toppings by thinly slicing ham or roast pork, julienned cucumber, julienned or shredded carrot, thinly sliced red bell pepper, bean sprouts, nori strips, chopped green onions, and any other preferred toppings.

Assemble the Cold Ramen (Hiyashi Chuka):
- Divide the chilled ramen noodles among serving bowls.
- Arrange the sliced ham or roast pork, cucumber, carrot, red bell pepper, bean sprouts, and other toppings over the noodles.

Drizzle with Sauce:
- Drizzle the prepared sauce over the toppings and noodles. You can adjust the amount of sauce based on your taste preference.

Garnish and Serve:
- Garnish the cold ramen with nori strips, chopped green onions, and sesame seeds.

Optional Additions:
- Add additional toppings like shredded omelet, shrimp, or other ingredients of your choice.

Serve Cold:
- Serve the Hiyashi Chuka immediately, allowing the refreshing and chilled flavors to shine.

Hiyashi Chuka is a versatile dish, and you can customize the toppings based on your preferences. It's a perfect option for a light and cooling meal during the warmer seasons.

Green Tea Ramen

Ingredients:

Ramen noodles: Use your preferred type, whether it's fresh, dried, or instant.
Green tea: You can use high-quality loose leaf green tea or green tea bags. Matcha powder is also an excellent choice for a more concentrated flavor.
Broth:
- 4 cups of vegetable or chicken broth (homemade or store-bought)
- 2 tablespoons soy sauce
- 1 tablespoon mirin (Japanese sweet rice wine)
- 1 tablespoon sesame oil
- 1 teaspoon grated ginger
- 2 cloves garlic, minced

Toppings:
- Sliced green onions
- Thinly sliced mushrooms
- Spinach or bok choy
- Bean sprouts
- Soft-boiled egg
- Nori (seaweed) sheets, cut into thin strips

Instructions:

Brew the Green Tea:
- Steep the green tea in hot water according to the package instructions. If using matcha powder, whisk it into a small amount of hot water until smooth.

Prepare the Broth:
- In a pot, combine the broth, soy sauce, mirin, sesame oil, grated ginger, and minced garlic. Bring the mixture to a simmer and let it cook for about 10-15 minutes to infuse the flavors.

Cook the Noodles:
- Cook the ramen noodles according to the package instructions. Drain and set aside.

Assemble the Ramen:
- Divide the cooked noodles among serving bowls.
- Pour the hot broth over the noodles.

- Add your desired toppings, such as sliced green onions, mushrooms, spinach, bean sprouts, and a soft-boiled egg.

Garnish and Serve:
- Drizzle some brewed green tea over the ramen as a finishing touch.
- Garnish with nori strips.

Feel free to customize the recipe based on your preferences. You can experiment with different types of green tea or adjust the broth ingredients to suit your taste. Green tea ramen offers a delightful fusion of flavors and a potential boost of antioxidants from the green tea.

Duck Ramen

Ingredients:

For the Broth:

    2 duck legs or breasts
    8 cups chicken or duck broth
    1 onion, peeled and halved
    3 cloves garlic, smashed
    1 piece of ginger (about 2 inches), sliced
    2 tablespoons soy sauce
    1 tablespoon mirin (Japanese sweet rice wine)
    1 tablespoon sake
    Salt and pepper to taste

For the Ramen:

    Ramen noodles (enough for your servings)
    Shredded duck meat (from the cooked duck legs/breasts)
    Bok choy, chopped
    Green onions, thinly sliced
    Shiitake mushrooms, sliced
    Soft-boiled eggs
    Nori (seaweed) sheets, cut into thin strips

Instructions:

1. Prepare the Duck:

    Pat the duck legs or breasts dry with paper towels and season with salt and pepper.
    In a large pot or Dutch oven, sear the duck on both sides over medium heat until browned. Remove any excess fat.
    Add the chicken or duck broth, onion, garlic, ginger, soy sauce, mirin, and sake to the pot. Bring to a boil and then reduce the heat to simmer.
    Cover and simmer for about 1.5 to 2 hours or until the duck is tender and easily falls off the bone.
    Once the duck is cooked, remove it from the pot, shred the meat, and discard the bones. Strain the broth to remove any solids, and season with additional soy sauce, salt, or pepper if needed.

2. Prepare the Ramen Components:

Cook the ramen noodles according to the package instructions. Drain and set aside.

In a separate pan, sauté the bok choy and shiitake mushrooms until tender.

Soft-boil the eggs and slice them in half.

3. Assemble the Duck Ramen:

Divide the cooked ramen noodles among serving bowls.

Pour the hot duck broth over the noodles.

Add shredded duck meat, sautéed bok choy, shiitake mushrooms, and green onions.

Place a soft-boiled egg half on top and garnish with nori strips.

Serve hot and enjoy your delicious duck ramen!

Feel free to customize the toppings and adjust the seasoning according to your preferences.

Duck ramen offers a unique and flavorful twist to the traditional ramen experience.

Beef Ramen

Ingredients:

For the Broth:

    1 pound beef bones (such as marrow or knuckle bones)
    8 cups beef broth (homemade or store-bought)
    1 onion, peeled and halved
    3 cloves garlic, minced
    1 piece of ginger (about 2 inches), sliced
    2 tablespoons soy sauce
    1 tablespoon mirin (Japanese sweet rice wine)
    1 tablespoon sake
    Salt and pepper to taste

For the Ramen:

    Ramen noodles (enough for your servings)
    Thinly sliced beef (such as sirloin or ribeye)
    Baby spinach or bok choy
    Green onions, thinly sliced
    Shiitake mushrooms, sliced
    Soft-boiled eggs
    Nori (seaweed) sheets, cut into thin strips
    Sesame oil (optional, for added flavor)

Instructions:

1. Prepare the Beef Broth:

    Roast the beef bones in the oven at 400°F (200°C) for about 30 minutes or until browned.
    In a large pot, combine the beef broth, roasted beef bones, onion, garlic, ginger, soy sauce, mirin, and sake.
    Bring the mixture to a boil and then reduce the heat to simmer. Skim off any impurities that rise to the surface.
    Simmer the broth for at least 1.5 to 2 hours to allow the flavors to meld. Season with salt and pepper to taste.
    Strain the broth to remove the bones and solids. Keep the broth warm.

2. Prepare the Ramen Components:

    Cook the ramen noodles according to the package instructions. Drain and set aside.
    In a separate pan, quickly sear the thinly sliced beef until just browned. Remove from heat and set aside.
    Sauté the baby spinach or bok choy until wilted.
    Soft-boil the eggs and slice them in half.

3. Assemble the Beef Ramen:

    Divide the cooked ramen noodles among serving bowls.
    Pour the hot beef broth over the noodles.
    Add the seared beef slices, sautéed greens, sliced shiitake mushrooms, green onions, and a soft-boiled egg half.
    Drizzle with sesame oil if desired, and garnish with nori strips.
    Serve hot and enjoy your flavorful beef ramen!

Feel free to customize the toppings and adjust the seasoning according to your preferences. Beef ramen provides a comforting and robust meal that's perfect for colder days.

Okinawa Soba

Ingredients:

For the Broth:

    8 cups dashi (Japanese fish and seaweed stock) or a combination of chicken and pork broth
    1/4 cup soy sauce
    1/4 cup sake
    2 tablespoons mirin (Japanese sweet rice wine)
    2 tablespoons brown sugar
    Salt to taste

For the Noodles:

    Okinawa soba noodles (substitute with udon or other thick noodles if unavailable)
    Water for boiling

Toppings:

    Thinly sliced green onions
    Red pickled ginger (beni shoga)
    Kamaboko (fish cake), sliced
    Rafute (slow-cooked pork belly), sliced (optional)
    Shiitake mushrooms, sliced and sautéed
    Bonito flakes (katsuobushi)

Instructions:

1. Prepare the Broth:

    In a large pot, combine the dashi or broth, soy sauce, sake, mirin, and brown sugar. Bring to a simmer over medium heat.
    Adjust the seasoning with salt to taste. Keep the broth warm while preparing the other components.

2. Cook the Noodles:

    Boil water in a separate pot and cook the Okinawa soba noodles according to the package instructions.

Drain the noodles and rinse them under cold water to remove excess starch.

3. Assemble Okinawa Soba:

> Divide the cooked noodles among serving bowls.
> Pour the hot broth over the noodles.
> Arrange the toppings on the noodles, including sliced green onions, red pickled ginger, kamaboko, rafute (if using), sautéed shiitake mushrooms, and bonito flakes.
> Serve immediately and enjoy your Okinawa soba!

Note: Rafute is a traditional Okinawan dish made by slowly simmering pork belly in soy sauce, sake, and sugar until it becomes tender. If you decide to include it, you can prepare it separately and slice it to add as a topping.

Feel free to customize the toppings based on your preferences. Okinawa soba offers a delicious blend of flavors and textures, making it a comforting and unique noodle dish.

Clam Ramen

Ingredients:

For the Broth:

    1 pound fresh clams (such as littleneck or Manila clams), scrubbed and cleaned
    8 cups seafood or chicken broth
    1 cup water
    1 onion, peeled and sliced
    3 cloves garlic, minced
    1 piece of ginger (about 2 inches), sliced
    2 tablespoons soy sauce
    1 tablespoon mirin (Japanese sweet rice wine)
    1 tablespoon sake
    Salt and pepper to taste

For the Ramen:

    Ramen noodles (enough for your servings)
    Clam meat (reserved from cooked clams)
    Baby bok choy, chopped
    Green onions, thinly sliced
    Shiitake mushrooms, sliced
    Nori (seaweed) sheets, cut into thin strips
    Sesame oil (optional, for added flavor)

Instructions:

1. Prepare the Clams and Broth:

    Rinse the clams thoroughly under cold water to remove any sand or debris.
    In a large pot, combine the broth, water, sliced onion, minced garlic, sliced ginger, soy sauce, mirin, and sake.
    Bring the broth to a simmer over medium heat. Add the cleaned clams and cover the pot.
    Cook until the clams open, usually 5-7 minutes. Discard any clams that do not open.
    Once the clams are cooked, remove them from the pot, and reserve the clam meat.
    Strain the broth to remove any solids.
    Season the broth with salt and pepper to taste. Keep the broth warm.

2. Prepare the Ramen Components:

Cook the ramen noodles according to the package instructions. Drain and set aside.

In a separate pan, sauté the baby bok choy and shiitake mushrooms until tender.

3. Assemble the Clam Ramen:

Divide the cooked ramen noodles among serving bowls.

Pour the hot clam broth over the noodles.

Add the sautéed baby bok choy, sliced shiitake mushrooms, reserved clam meat, and green onions.

Drizzle with sesame oil if desired and garnish with nori strips.

Serve hot and enjoy your flavorful clam ramen!

Feel free to customize the toppings and adjust the seasoning according to your preferences.

Clam ramen provides a light yet savory seafood twist to the classic ramen experience.

Cilantro Lime Ramen

Ingredients:

For the Broth:

    4 cups vegetable or chicken broth
    1 cup water
    1/4 cup soy sauce
    2 tablespoons sesame oil
    2 tablespoons rice vinegar
    2 tablespoons lime juice
    2 teaspoons sugar
    2 cloves garlic, minced
    1 piece of ginger (about 1 inch), grated
    Salt and pepper to taste

For the Ramen:

    Ramen noodles (enough for your servings)
    Fresh cilantro, chopped
    Green onions, thinly sliced
    Red chili flakes (optional, for heat)
    Lime wedges for serving

Instructions:

1. Prepare the Broth:

    In a pot, combine the vegetable or chicken broth, water, soy sauce, sesame oil, rice vinegar, lime juice, sugar, minced garlic, and grated ginger.
    Bring the mixture to a simmer over medium heat. Allow it to simmer for about 10-15 minutes to let the flavors meld.
    Season the broth with salt and pepper to taste. Adjust the soy sauce, lime juice, or sugar if needed for your preferred balance of flavors.

2. Cook the Ramen Noodles:

    Cook the ramen noodles according to the package instructions. Drain and set aside.

3. Assemble the Cilantro Lime Ramen:

    Divide the cooked ramen noodles among serving bowls.

Pour the hot cilantro lime broth over the noodles.
Sprinkle chopped fresh cilantro, green onions, and red chili flakes (if using) on top.
Serve with lime wedges on the side for an extra burst of lime flavor.
Enjoy your refreshing cilantro lime ramen!

Feel free to customize the recipe by adding protein such as grilled chicken, tofu, or shrimp. The combination of cilantro and lime adds a bright and citrusy element to the ramen, making it a perfect choice for a light and flavorful meal.

Teriyaki Chicken Ramen

Ingredients:

For the Teriyaki Chicken:

- 2 boneless, skinless chicken breasts, sliced into strips
- 1/4 cup soy sauce
- 2 tablespoons mirin (Japanese sweet rice wine)
- 2 tablespoons sake (or dry sherry)
- 2 tablespoons brown sugar
- 1 tablespoon honey
- 2 cloves garlic, minced
- 1 teaspoon grated ginger
- 1 tablespoon vegetable oil for cooking

For the Ramen:

- Ramen noodles (enough for your servings)
- 4 cups chicken broth
- 2 tablespoons soy sauce
- 1 tablespoon mirin
- 1 tablespoon sesame oil
- 1 tablespoon rice vinegar
- 1 teaspoon grated ginger
- Sliced green onions for garnish
- Sesame seeds for garnish (optional)
- Red chili flakes for added heat (optional)

Instructions:

For the Teriyaki Chicken:

In a bowl, mix together soy sauce, mirin, sake, brown sugar, honey, minced garlic, and grated ginger to make the teriyaki sauce.
Marinate the chicken strips in half of the teriyaki sauce for at least 30 minutes.
Heat vegetable oil in a skillet over medium-high heat. Cook the marinated chicken strips until fully cooked and caramelized, about 5-7 minutes. Reserve the remaining teriyaki sauce for later.

For the Ramen:

In a pot, combine chicken broth, soy sauce, mirin, sesame oil, rice vinegar, and grated ginger. Bring the mixture to a simmer.

Cook the ramen noodles according to the package instructions. Drain and set aside.

Assemble the ramen bowls by placing cooked noodles in each serving bowl.

Pour the hot broth over the noodles.

Top with teriyaki chicken strips.

Garnish with sliced green onions, sesame seeds (if using), and red chili flakes for added heat.

Drizzle the remaining teriyaki sauce over the chicken and noodles.

Serve immediately and enjoy your teriyaki chicken ramen!

Feel free to customize the recipe by adding vegetables like bok choy, spinach, or mushrooms. This flavorful and savory dish brings together the best of teriyaki and ramen in a delightful combination.

Shrimp Tempura Ramen

Ingredients:

For the Shrimp Tempura:

- 12 large shrimp, peeled and deveined
- 1 cup tempura flour (or a mixture of all-purpose flour and cornstarch)
- 1 cup ice-cold water
- Vegetable oil for frying

For the Ramen:

- Ramen noodles (enough for your servings)
- 4 cups shrimp or vegetable broth
- 2 tablespoons soy sauce
- 1 tablespoon mirin (Japanese sweet rice wine)
- 1 tablespoon sake
- 1 teaspoon sesame oil
- 1 teaspoon grated ginger
- Sliced green onions for garnish
- Nori (seaweed) sheets, cut into thin strips
- Sesame seeds for garnish

Instructions:

For the Shrimp Tempura:

- In a bowl, mix tempura flour with ice-cold water until just combined. The batter should be lumpy; do not overmix.
- Heat vegetable oil in a deep fryer or a large, deep pan to 350°F (180°C).
- Dip each shrimp into the tempura batter, ensuring they are evenly coated.
- Carefully place the battered shrimp into the hot oil and fry until golden brown and crispy. This usually takes 2-3 minutes per side.
- Remove the shrimp from the oil and place them on a paper towel to absorb excess oil.

For the Ramen:

- In a pot, combine shrimp or vegetable broth, soy sauce, mirin, sake, sesame oil, and grated ginger. Bring the mixture to a simmer.
- Cook the ramen noodles according to the package instructions. Drain and set aside.
- Assemble the ramen bowls by placing cooked noodles in each serving bowl.

Pour the hot broth over the noodles.
Top with shrimp tempura.
Garnish with sliced green onions, nori strips, and sesame seeds.
Serve immediately, and enjoy your shrimp tempura ramen!

Feel free to customize the ramen by adding vegetables like sliced mushrooms, spinach, or bean sprouts. The crispy and flavorful shrimp tempura adds a delightful crunch to the ramen, creating a unique and satisfying meal.

Garlic Butter Ramen

Ingredients:

For the Ramen:

    Ramen noodles (enough for your servings)
    4 cups chicken or vegetable broth
    3 cloves garlic, minced
    2 tablespoons soy sauce
    1 tablespoon mirin (Japanese sweet rice wine)
    1 tablespoon sesame oil
    1 teaspoon grated ginger
    Salt and pepper to taste

For the Garlic Butter Sauce:

    4 tablespoons unsalted butter
    4 cloves garlic, minced
    1 tablespoon soy sauce
    1 teaspoon sesame oil

Optional Toppings:

    Sliced green onions
    Soft-boiled eggs
    Seaweed (nori) sheets, cut into thin strips
    Sesame seeds

Instructions:

For the Ramen:

    In a pot, bring the chicken or vegetable broth to a simmer over medium heat.
    Add minced garlic, soy sauce, mirin, sesame oil, grated ginger, salt, and pepper to the simmering broth. Let it cook for 10-15 minutes to allow the flavors to meld.
    Cook the ramen noodles according to the package instructions. Drain and set aside.

For the Garlic Butter Sauce:

    In a small saucepan, melt the unsalted butter over medium heat.
    Add minced garlic to the melted butter and sauté until fragrant and lightly golden.

Stir in soy sauce and sesame oil. Cook for an additional 1-2 minutes, ensuring the garlic doesn't burn.

Assemble the Garlic Butter Ramen:

> Divide the cooked ramen noodles among serving bowls.
> Pour the hot broth over the noodles.
> Drizzle the garlic butter sauce over the ramen.
> Optionally, add sliced green onions, soft-boiled eggs, nori strips, and sesame seeds as toppings.
> Serve immediately and enjoy your delicious garlic butter ramen!

Feel free to customize the recipe by adding your favorite vegetables or protein, such as sliced mushrooms, spinach, or grilled chicken. The combination of garlic, butter, and savory broth creates a comforting and indulgent bowl of ramen.

Yuzu Ramen

Ingredients:

For the Broth:

    4 cups vegetable or chicken broth
    1 cup water
    2 tablespoons soy sauce
    1 tablespoon mirin (Japanese sweet rice wine)
    1 tablespoon sake
    1 tablespoon yuzu juice (fresh or bottled)
    1 teaspoon grated yuzu zest (optional)
    1 tablespoon sesame oil
    2 cloves garlic, minced
    1 piece of ginger (about 1 inch), sliced
    Salt and pepper to taste

For the Ramen:

    Ramen noodles (enough for your servings)
    Sliced shiitake mushrooms
    Baby spinach or bok choy, chopped
    Green onions, thinly sliced
    Yuzu slices for garnish
    Nori (seaweed) sheets, cut into thin strips
    Sesame seeds for garnish

Instructions:

For the Broth:

    In a pot, combine vegetable or chicken broth, water, soy sauce, mirin, sake, yuzu juice, yuzu zest (if using), sesame oil, minced garlic, and sliced ginger.
    Bring the mixture to a simmer over medium heat. Allow it to simmer for about 10-15 minutes to let the flavors meld.
    Season the broth with salt and pepper to taste. Adjust the soy sauce, yuzu juice, or mirin if needed for your preferred balance of flavors.

For the Ramen:

Cook the ramen noodles according to the package instructions. Drain and set aside.

In the same pot as the broth, add sliced shiitake mushrooms and chopped baby spinach or bok choy. Let them simmer until they are tender.

Assemble Yuzu Ramen:

Divide the cooked ramen noodles among serving bowls.
Pour the hot yuzu-infused broth with vegetables over the noodles.
Garnish with sliced green onions, yuzu slices, nori strips, and sesame seeds.
Serve immediately and enjoy your unique and citrusy yuzu ramen!

Feel free to customize the recipe by adding your preferred protein, such as tofu, shrimp, or chicken. Yuzu ramen offers a refreshing and aromatic twist to the classic ramen experience.

Sukiyaki Ramen

Ingredients:

For the Sukiyaki Broth:

- 4 cups dashi (Japanese fish and seaweed stock)
- 1/2 cup soy sauce
- 1/4 cup mirin (Japanese sweet rice wine)
- 2 tablespoons sake
- 2 tablespoons sugar
- 2 cloves garlic, minced
- 1 piece of ginger (about 2 inches), sliced
- 1 tablespoon vegetable oil

For the Ramen:

- Ramen noodles (enough for your servings)
- Thinly sliced beef (such as ribeye or sirloin)
- Tofu, cut into cubes
- Shungiku (edible chrysanthemum leaves) or spinach, washed and trimmed
- Napa cabbage, sliced
- Shiitake mushrooms, sliced
- Green onions, thinly sliced
- Kamaboko (fish cake), sliced
- Soft-boiled eggs (optional)
- Sesame seeds for garnish
- Shichimi togarashi (Japanese seven-spice blend) for added spice (optional)

Instructions:

For the Sukiyaki Broth:

In a large pot or deep skillet, heat the vegetable oil over medium heat. Add minced garlic and sliced ginger, sautéing until fragrant.

Pour in the dashi, soy sauce, mirin, sake, and sugar. Bring the mixture to a simmer.

Add the thinly sliced beef to the simmering broth. Cook for 1-2 minutes until the beef is just cooked.

Add tofu cubes, shungiku or spinach, sliced Napa cabbage, and shiitake mushrooms to the pot. Simmer until the vegetables are tender.

For the Ramen:

- Cook the ramen noodles according to the package instructions. Drain and set aside.
- Assemble the sukiyaki ramen bowls by placing cooked noodles in each serving bowl.
- Ladle the sukiyaki broth with beef and vegetables over the noodles.
- Top with sliced green onions, kamaboko, and soft-boiled eggs if desired.
- Sprinkle sesame seeds and shichimi togarashi over the ramen for added flavor.
- Serve immediately and enjoy your sukiyaki ramen!

Feel free to customize the recipe by adding other ingredients commonly found in sukiyaki, such as enoki mushrooms or shirataki noodles. Sukiyaki ramen provides a rich and savory hot pot experience in the form of comforting ramen.

Shrimp and Pork Wonton Ramen

Ingredients:

For the Wontons:

    1/2 pound shrimp, peeled and deveined
    1/2 pound ground pork
    2 cloves garlic, minced
    1 tablespoon soy sauce
    1 tablespoon oyster sauce
    1 tablespoon sesame oil
    1 green onion, finely chopped
    Wonton wrappers

For the Ramen Broth:

    6 cups chicken or pork broth
    2 tablespoons soy sauce
    1 tablespoon mirin (Japanese sweet rice wine)
    1 tablespoon sake
    2 cloves garlic, minced
    1 piece of ginger (about 2 inches), sliced
    Salt and pepper to taste

Other Ramen Ingredients:

    Ramen noodles (enough for your servings)
    Baby bok choy or spinach, washed and trimmed
    Green onions, thinly sliced
    Nori (seaweed) sheets, cut into thin strips
    Sesame seeds for garnish
    Soft-boiled eggs (optional)

Instructions:

For the Wontons:

    In a food processor, combine shrimp, ground pork, minced garlic, soy sauce, oyster sauce, sesame oil, and chopped green onion. Pulse until the mixture is well combined but still has some texture.

Place a small amount of the filling in the center of a wonton wrapper. Moisten the edges of the wrapper with water, then fold it over to form a triangle. Press the edges to seal.

Bring the two corners of the triangle together and press to seal, creating a classic wonton shape. Repeat with the remaining filling and wrappers.

For the Ramen Broth:

In a pot, combine chicken or pork broth, soy sauce, mirin, sake, minced garlic, and sliced ginger. Bring the mixture to a simmer over medium heat.

Season the broth with salt and pepper to taste. Let it simmer for about 10-15 minutes to allow the flavors to meld.

To Assemble the Shrimp and Pork Wonton Ramen:

Cook the ramen noodles according to the package instructions. Drain and set aside.

In the same pot as the broth, add baby bok choy or spinach and simmer until just tender.

Carefully add the wontons to the simmering broth and cook until they float to the surface, indicating they are cooked.

Divide the cooked ramen noodles among serving bowls.

Ladle the hot broth with wontons and vegetables over the noodles.

Top with sliced green onions, nori strips, sesame seeds, and soft-boiled eggs if desired.

Serve immediately and enjoy your delicious shrimp and pork wonton ramen!

Feel free to customize the recipe by adding other ingredients like sliced mushrooms or bamboo shoots. Shrimp and pork wonton ramen offers a rich and satisfying bowl with the delicate flavors of the filling and the comforting warmth of the broth.

Udon Noodle Soup

Ingredients:

For the Broth:

    6 cups dashi (Japanese fish and seaweed stock) or a combination of chicken and vegetable broth
    1/4 cup soy sauce
    2 tablespoons mirin (Japanese sweet rice wine)
    1 tablespoon sake
    1 tablespoon sugar
    Salt to taste

For the Udon Noodles:

    Fresh or frozen udon noodles (enough for your servings)
    Water for boiling

Toppings:

    Sliced green onions
    Kamaboko (fish cake), sliced
    Shiitake mushrooms, sliced and sautéed
    Baby bok choy or spinach, blanched
    Tempura flakes (tenkasu)
    Nori (seaweed) sheets, cut into thin strips
    Sesame seeds for garnish

Instructions:

For the Broth:

    In a pot, combine dashi (or broth), soy sauce, mirin, sake, sugar, and salt. Bring the mixture to a simmer over medium heat. Allow it to simmer for about 10-15 minutes to let the flavors meld.
    Adjust the seasoning with salt or sugar to taste.

For the Udon Noodles:

Boil water in a separate pot and cook the udon noodles according to the package instructions. Fresh udon noodles typically cook quickly, while frozen udon may take a bit longer.

Drain the udon noodles and rinse them under cold water to remove excess starch.

Assemble Udon Noodle Soup:

Divide the cooked udon noodles among serving bowls.

Pour the hot broth over the noodles.

Arrange your desired toppings on the noodles, such as sliced green onions, kamaboko, sautéed shiitake mushrooms, blanched baby bok choy or spinach, tempura flakes, nori strips, and sesame seeds.

Serve immediately and enjoy your comforting udon noodle soup!

Feel free to customize the toppings based on your preferences. You can also add protein like sliced chicken, tofu, or shrimp for a heartier version. Udon noodle soup is versatile and can be adjusted to suit your taste, making it a perfect warming dish for any occasion.

Vegan Ramen

Ingredients:

For the Broth:

    8 cups vegetable broth
    1 onion, peeled and halved
    4 cloves garlic, minced
    1 piece of ginger (about 2 inches), sliced
    2 tablespoons soy sauce
    1 tablespoon miso paste
    1 tablespoon sesame oil
    1 tablespoon mirin (optional)
    1 teaspoon agave syrup or another sweetener
    Salt and pepper to taste

For the Ramen:

    Ramen noodles (enough for your servings)
    Assorted vegetables (such as sliced mushrooms, bok choy, shredded carrots, snow peas, and bean sprouts)
    Tofu, cubed and pan-fried
    Green onions, thinly sliced
    Nori (seaweed) sheets, cut into thin strips
    Sesame seeds for garnish

Instructions:

For the Broth:

    In a large pot, combine vegetable broth, onion, garlic, ginger, soy sauce, miso paste, sesame oil, mirin (if using), agave syrup, salt, and pepper.
    Bring the mixture to a boil, then reduce the heat to simmer. Allow it to simmer for about 20-30 minutes to let the flavors meld.
    Taste and adjust the seasoning if needed. Remove the onion, garlic, and ginger pieces from the broth.

For the Ramen:

    Cook the ramen noodles according to the package instructions. Drain and set aside.
    In a separate pan, sauté the assorted vegetables until they are tender-crisp.

Pan-fry the tofu until it's golden brown on all sides.

Assemble Vegan Ramen:

Divide the cooked ramen noodles among serving bowls.
Pour the hot broth over the noodles.
Add the sautéed vegetables and pan-fried tofu on top.
Garnish with sliced green onions, nori strips, and sesame seeds.
Serve immediately and enjoy your delicious vegan ramen!

Feel free to customize the recipe by adding your favorite vegetables and protein sources. Vegan ramen is a versatile and satisfying dish that provides the comforting flavors of traditional ramen without animal products.

Truffle Ramen

Ingredients:

For the Truffle Broth:

    4 cups vegetable or mushroom broth
    1 tablespoon truffle oil
    2 tablespoons soy sauce
    1 tablespoon mirin (Japanese sweet rice wine)
    1 tablespoon sake
    2 cloves garlic, minced
    1 piece of ginger (about 1 inch), sliced
    Salt and pepper to taste

For the Ramen:

    Ramen noodles (enough for your servings)
    Sliced shiitake mushrooms
    Baby spinach or bok choy, washed and trimmed
    Green onions, thinly sliced
    Truffle-infused oil for drizzling
    Truffle slices or truffle salt for garnish (optional)
    Sesame seeds for garnish

Instructions:

For the Truffle Broth:

    In a pot, combine vegetable or mushroom broth, truffle oil, soy sauce, mirin, sake, minced garlic, and sliced ginger.
    Bring the mixture to a simmer over medium heat. Allow it to simmer for about 10-15 minutes to let the flavors meld.
    Season the broth with salt and pepper to taste. Adjust the soy sauce, truffle oil, or mirin if needed for your preferred balance of flavors.

For the Ramen:

    Cook the ramen noodles according to the package instructions. Drain and set aside.
    In the same pot as the broth, add sliced shiitake mushrooms and baby spinach or bok choy. Let them simmer until just tender.

Assemble Truffle Ramen:

- Divide the cooked ramen noodles among serving bowls.
- Pour the hot truffle-infused broth with vegetables over the noodles.
- Drizzle with truffle-infused oil for an extra burst of flavor.
- Top with sliced green onions and sesame seeds.
- Optionally, garnish with truffle slices or sprinkle truffle salt over the ramen.
- Serve immediately and enjoy your luxurious truffle ramen!

Feel free to customize the recipe by adding other ingredients like tofu, seaweed, or bean sprouts. Truffle ramen provides a rich and earthy twist to the classic ramen experience, making it a perfect indulgence for special occasions.

Char Siu Ramen

Ingredients:

For the Char Siu:

    1 pound pork belly or pork shoulder
    2 tablespoons hoisin sauce
    2 tablespoons soy sauce
    2 tablespoons oyster sauce
    2 tablespoons mirin (Japanese sweet rice wine)
    1 tablespoon honey
    2 cloves garlic, minced
    1 tablespoon grated ginger
    1 teaspoon Chinese five-spice powder

For the Ramen:

    4 portions of ramen noodles (fresh or dried)
    6 cups chicken or pork broth
    2 tablespoons soy sauce
    1 tablespoon mirin
    1 tablespoon sake
    1 tablespoon sesame oil
    2 cloves garlic, minced
    1 piece of ginger (about 1 inch), sliced
    Sliced green onions for garnish
    Nori (seaweed) sheets, cut into thin strips
    Sesame seeds for garnish

Instructions:

For the Char Siu:

    Mix hoisin sauce, soy sauce, oyster sauce, mirin, honey, minced garlic, grated ginger, and Chinese five-spice powder in a bowl to create the marinade.
    Place the pork in a zip-top bag or shallow dish and coat it evenly with the marinade.
    Marinate in the refrigerator for at least 4 hours or overnight.
    Preheat your oven to 350°F (175°C). Remove the pork from the marinade and place it on a wire rack set over a baking sheet.

Roast the pork in the oven for about 45-60 minutes, or until it reaches an internal temperature of 145°F (63°C). Baste with the marinade every 15-20 minutes for a glossy finish.

Once cooked, let the pork rest for a few minutes before slicing it thinly.

For the Ramen:

In a pot, combine chicken or pork broth, soy sauce, mirin, sake, sesame oil, minced garlic, and sliced ginger. Bring the mixture to a simmer over medium heat.

Cook the ramen noodles according to the package instructions. Drain and set aside.

Assemble Char Siu Ramen:

Divide the cooked ramen noodles among serving bowls.

Pour the hot broth over the noodles.

Arrange slices of char siu on top of the noodles.

Garnish with sliced green onions, nori strips, and sesame seeds.

Serve immediately and enjoy your delicious char siu ramen!

Feel free to customize the recipe by adding other toppings like boiled eggs, bamboo shoots, or bean sprouts. Char siu ramen brings together the rich flavors of Chinese barbecue pork with the comforting appeal of Japanese ramen.

Egg Drop Ramen

Ingredients:

For the Broth:

    4 cups chicken or vegetable broth
    1 tablespoon soy sauce
    1 tablespoon mirin (Japanese sweet rice wine)
    1 tablespoon sake
    1 teaspoon sesame oil
    2 cloves garlic, minced
    1 piece of ginger (about 1 inch), sliced
    Salt and pepper to taste

For the Ramen:

    Ramen noodles (enough for your servings)
    2-3 large eggs, beaten
    Sliced green onions for garnish
    Nori (seaweed) sheets, cut into thin strips
    Sesame seeds for garnish

Instructions:

For the Broth:

    In a pot, combine chicken or vegetable broth, soy sauce, mirin, sake, sesame oil, minced garlic, and sliced ginger.
    Bring the mixture to a simmer over medium heat. Allow it to simmer for about 10-15 minutes to let the flavors meld.
    Season the broth with salt and pepper to taste. Adjust the soy sauce, mirin, or sesame oil if needed for your preferred balance of flavors.

For the Ramen:

    Cook the ramen noodles according to the package instructions. Drain and set aside. While the noodles are cooking, slowly pour the beaten eggs into the simmering broth in a thin, steady stream, stirring gently with chopsticks or a fork to create silky egg ribbons. The eggs will cook almost instantly.

Assemble Egg Drop Ramen:

Divide the cooked ramen noodles among serving bowls.
Pour the hot egg-drop broth over the noodles.
Garnish with sliced green onions, nori strips, and sesame seeds.
Serve immediately and enjoy your comforting egg drop ramen!

Feel free to customize the recipe by adding other ingredients like tofu, mushrooms, or spinach.

The silky texture of the egg ribbons adds a delightful richness to the ramen, making it a comforting and satisfying dish.

Lemon Soy Ramen

Ingredients:

For the Broth:

    4 cups vegetable or chicken broth
    1/4 cup soy sauce
    2 tablespoons mirin (Japanese sweet rice wine)
    1 tablespoon sesame oil
    1 tablespoon lemon juice
    1 teaspoon grated lemon zest
    2 cloves garlic, minced
    1 piece of ginger (about 1 inch), sliced
    Salt and pepper to taste

For the Ramen:

    Ramen noodles (enough for your servings)
    Sliced mushrooms
    Baby spinach or bok choy, washed and trimmed
    Green onions, thinly sliced
    Red chili flakes for added heat (optional)
    Lemon wedges for serving

Instructions:

For the Broth:

    In a pot, combine vegetable or chicken broth, soy sauce, mirin, sesame oil, lemon juice, grated lemon zest, minced garlic, and sliced ginger.
    Bring the mixture to a simmer over medium heat. Allow it to simmer for about 10-15 minutes to let the flavors meld.
    Season the broth with salt and pepper to taste. Adjust the soy sauce, lemon juice, or mirin if needed for your preferred balance of flavors.

For the Ramen:

    Cook the ramen noodles according to the package instructions. Drain and set aside.
    In the same pot as the broth, add sliced mushrooms and baby spinach or bok choy. Let them simmer until just tender.

Assemble Lemon Soy Ramen:

    Divide the cooked ramen noodles among serving bowls.
    Pour the hot lemon-infused broth with vegetables over the noodles.
    Sprinkle sliced green onions and red chili flakes (if using) on top.
    Serve with lemon wedges on the side for an extra burst of citrus flavor.
    Enjoy your refreshing and zesty lemon soy ramen!

Feel free to customize the recipe by adding protein such as tofu, shrimp, or grilled chicken. The combination of lemon and soy creates a unique and vibrant flavor profile, making this ramen a perfect choice for a light and flavorful meal.

Braised Pork Belly Ramen

Ingredients:

For the Braised Pork Belly:

    1.5 to 2 pounds pork belly, skin on
    1/2 cup soy sauce
    1/4 cup sake
    1/4 cup mirin (Japanese sweet rice wine)
    1/4 cup brown sugar
    4 cloves garlic, minced
    2 tablespoons ginger, grated
    2 green onions, chopped
    1 tablespoon vegetable oil

For the Ramen Broth:

    6 cups chicken or pork broth
    2 tablespoons soy sauce
    1 tablespoon mirin
    1 tablespoon sake
    1 tablespoon sesame oil
    2 cloves garlic, minced
    1 piece of ginger (about 2 inches), sliced
    Salt and pepper to taste

For the Ramen:

    Ramen noodles (enough for your servings)
    Baby bok choy, washed and trimmed
    Sliced mushrooms
    Soft-boiled eggs (optional)
    Green onions, thinly sliced
    Sesame seeds for garnish
    Nori (seaweed) sheets, cut into thin strips

Instructions:

For the Braised Pork Belly:

    Preheat the oven to 325°F (163°C).

In a bowl, mix together soy sauce, sake, mirin, brown sugar, minced garlic, grated ginger, and chopped green onions to create the marinade.

Heat vegetable oil in an oven-safe pot or Dutch oven over medium-high heat.

Sear the pork belly on all sides until browned.

Pour the marinade over the pork belly.

Cover the pot and transfer it to the preheated oven. Braise for 2 to 2.5 hours or until the pork is tender and easily pulls apart.

Once done, remove the pork from the oven and let it rest. Slice the pork belly into thin pieces.

For the Ramen Broth:

In a pot, combine chicken or pork broth, soy sauce, mirin, sake, sesame oil, minced garlic, and sliced ginger.

Bring the mixture to a simmer over medium heat. Allow it to simmer for about 10-15 minutes to let the flavors meld.

Season the broth with salt and pepper to taste. Adjust the soy sauce, mirin, or sesame oil if needed.

For the Ramen:

Cook the ramen noodles according to the package instructions. Drain and set aside.

In the same pot as the broth, add baby bok choy and sliced mushrooms. Simmer until they are just tender.

Assemble Braised Pork Belly Ramen:

Divide the cooked ramen noodles among serving bowls.

Pour the hot broth with vegetables over the noodles.

Arrange slices of braised pork belly on top.

If desired, add soft-boiled eggs, sliced green onions, sesame seeds, and nori strips as garnish.

Serve immediately and enjoy your luxurious braised pork belly ramen!

Feel free to customize the recipe by adding other toppings like corn, bamboo shoots, or bean sprouts. Braised pork belly ramen is a hearty and flavorful dish that brings together the succulence of the pork belly with the comforting warmth of ramen.

Crab Ramen

Ingredients:

For the Crab Broth:

    4 cups seafood or chicken broth
    1 pound crab legs or crab meat (fresh or frozen)
    1 onion, chopped
    2 cloves garlic, minced
    1 piece of ginger (about 2 inches), sliced
    2 tablespoons soy sauce
    1 tablespoon mirin (Japanese sweet rice wine)
    1 tablespoon sake
    1 teaspoon sesame oil
    Salt and pepper to taste

For the Ramen:

    Ramen noodles (enough for your servings)
    Crab meat (if not using crab legs for the broth)
    Baby bok choy, washed and trimmed
    Sliced shiitake mushrooms
    Green onions, thinly sliced
    Nori (seaweed) sheets, cut into thin strips
    Sesame seeds for garnish

Instructions:

For the Crab Broth:

    In a pot, combine seafood or chicken broth, crab legs or crab meat, chopped onion, minced garlic, sliced ginger, soy sauce, mirin, sake, and sesame oil.
    Bring the mixture to a simmer over medium heat. Allow it to simmer for about 20-30 minutes to extract flavors from the crab.
    Strain the broth to remove solids, leaving a clear crab-infused broth. Discard the solids.
    Season the broth with salt and pepper to taste. Adjust the soy sauce, mirin, or sesame oil if needed.

For the Ramen:

    Cook the ramen noodles according to the package instructions. Drain and set aside.

In the same pot as the broth, add baby bok choy and sliced shiitake mushrooms. Simmer until they are just tender.

Assemble Crab Ramen:

Divide the cooked ramen noodles among serving bowls.
Pour the hot crab-infused broth with vegetables over the noodles.
If using crab legs, carefully remove the crab meat from the shells and add it to the ramen. If using crab meat, add it directly to the ramen.
Garnish with sliced green onions, nori strips, and sesame seeds.
Serve immediately and enjoy your delicious crab ramen!

Feel free to customize the recipe by adding other ingredients like corn, bamboo shoots, or bean sprouts. Crab ramen offers a unique and delicate seafood twist to the classic ramen experience.

Gyoza Ramen

Ingredients:

For the Gyoza:

    1 pound ground pork or chicken
    2 cups finely shredded cabbage
    2 green onions, finely chopped
    2 cloves garlic, minced
    1 tablespoon ginger, grated
    2 tablespoons soy sauce
    1 tablespoon sesame oil
    1 teaspoon sugar
    Gyoza wrappers (round or square)
    Water for sealing the wrappers
    Vegetable oil for pan-frying

For the Ramen Broth:

    6 cups chicken or vegetable broth
    2 tablespoons soy sauce
    1 tablespoon mirin (Japanese sweet rice wine)
    1 tablespoon sake
    1 tablespoon sesame oil
    2 cloves garlic, minced
    1 piece of ginger (about 2 inches), sliced
    Salt and pepper to taste

For the Ramen:

    Ramen noodles (enough for your servings)
    Baby bok choy or spinach, washed and trimmed
    Sliced shiitake mushrooms
    Sliced green onions for garnish
    Nori (seaweed) sheets, cut into thin strips
    Sesame seeds for garnish

Instructions:

For the Gyoza:

In a bowl, combine ground pork or chicken, shredded cabbage, chopped green onions, minced garlic, grated ginger, soy sauce, sesame oil, and sugar. Mix well.

Place a small amount of the filling in the center of a gyoza wrapper.

Moisten the edges of the wrapper with water, then fold it over to create a half-moon shape. Pinch and pleat the edges to seal.

Heat vegetable oil in a pan over medium-high heat. Place the gyoza in the pan and cook until the bottoms are golden brown.

Add water to the pan, cover, and steam the gyoza until the filling is cooked through and the wrappers are translucent.

Remove the lid and let the gyoza continue cooking until the water evaporates, and the bottoms become crispy again.

For the Ramen Broth:

In a pot, combine chicken or vegetable broth, soy sauce, mirin, sake, sesame oil, minced garlic, and sliced ginger.

Bring the mixture to a simmer over medium heat. Allow it to simmer for about 10-15 minutes to let the flavors meld.

Season the broth with salt and pepper to taste. Adjust the soy sauce, mirin, or sesame oil if needed.

For the Ramen:

Cook the ramen noodles according to the package instructions. Drain and set aside.

In the same pot as the broth, add baby bok choy or spinach and sliced shiitake mushrooms. Simmer until they are just tender.

Assemble Gyoza Ramen:

Divide the cooked ramen noodles among serving bowls.

Pour the hot broth with vegetables over the noodles.

Arrange gyoza on top of the ramen.

Garnish with sliced green onions, nori strips, and sesame seeds.

Serve immediately and enjoy your delicious gyoza ramen!

Feel free to customize the recipe by adding other ingredients like corn, bamboo shoots, or bean sprouts. Gyoza ramen brings together the comforting flavors of ramen with the savory goodness of Japanese dumplings.

Green Curry Ramen

Ingredients:

For the Green Curry Broth:

    4 cups vegetable or chicken broth
    2 tablespoons green curry paste
    1 can (14 ounces) coconut milk
    2 tablespoons soy sauce
    1 tablespoon brown sugar
    1 tablespoon lime juice
    2 cloves garlic, minced
    1 piece of ginger (about 1 inch), grated
    1 stalk lemongrass, smashed
    Salt and pepper to taste

For the Ramen:

    Ramen noodles (enough for your servings)
    Sliced bell peppers (assorted colors)
    Sliced carrots
    Snap peas, trimmed
    Tofu, cubed and pan-fried (optional protein)
    Fresh cilantro leaves for garnish
    Lime wedges for serving
    Red chili flakes or fresh Thai chilies for added heat (optional)
    Sesame seeds for garnish

Instructions:

For the Green Curry Broth:

    In a pot, combine vegetable or chicken broth, green curry paste, coconut milk, soy sauce, brown sugar, lime juice, minced garlic, grated ginger, and smashed lemongrass.
    Bring the mixture to a simmer over medium heat. Allow it to simmer for about 15-20 minutes to let the flavors meld.
    Season the broth with salt and pepper to taste. Adjust the soy sauce, brown sugar, or lime juice if needed.
    Remove the lemongrass stalk and discard.

For the Ramen:

> Cook the ramen noodles according to the package instructions. Drain and set aside.
> In the same pot as the broth, add sliced bell peppers, sliced carrots, and snap peas. Simmer until the vegetables are just tender.
> If using tofu, pan-fry the tofu cubes until golden brown.

Assemble Green Curry Ramen:

> Divide the cooked ramen noodles among serving bowls.
> Pour the hot green curry broth with vegetables over the noodles.
> Top with tofu cubes if using.
> Garnish with fresh cilantro leaves, lime wedges, red chili flakes (if using), and sesame seeds.
> Serve immediately and enjoy your flavorful green curry ramen!

Feel free to customize the recipe by adding other ingredients like baby corn, bamboo shoots, or bean sprouts. Green curry ramen offers a fusion of Thai and Japanese flavors, creating a unique and delicious bowl of comfort.

Peanut Sesame Ramen

Ingredients:

For the Peanut Sesame Sauce:

    1/2 cup creamy peanut butter
    2 tablespoons soy sauce
    2 tablespoons sesame oil
    1 tablespoon rice vinegar
    1 tablespoon honey or maple syrup
    2 cloves garlic, minced
    1 piece of ginger (about 1 inch), grated
    1 teaspoon chili oil or Sriracha (adjust to taste)
    1/4 cup warm water (to thin the sauce)

For the Ramen:

    Ramen noodles (enough for your servings)
    Sliced bell peppers (assorted colors)
    Shredded carrots
    Bean sprouts
    Green onions, thinly sliced
    Sesame seeds for garnish
    Cilantro leaves for garnish
    Lime wedges for serving

Instructions:

For the Peanut Sesame Sauce:

    In a bowl, whisk together creamy peanut butter, soy sauce, sesame oil, rice vinegar, honey or maple syrup, minced garlic, grated ginger, and chili oil or Sriracha.
    Add warm water gradually, stirring continuously, until you achieve a smooth and pourable consistency. Adjust the water as needed.

For the Ramen:

    Cook the ramen noodles according to the package instructions. Drain and set aside.

In a pot, bring water to a boil and blanch the sliced bell peppers, shredded carrots, and bean sprouts for about 1-2 minutes until slightly tender. Drain and set aside.

Assemble Peanut Sesame Ramen:

- Divide the cooked ramen noodles among serving bowls.
- Pour the peanut sesame sauce over the noodles.
- Add the blanched vegetables on top of the noodles.
- Garnish with sliced green onions, sesame seeds, cilantro leaves, and lime wedges.
- Toss everything together before serving, ensuring the noodles are coated in the peanut sesame sauce.
- Serve immediately and enjoy your flavorful peanut sesame ramen!

Feel free to customize the recipe by adding other ingredients like tofu, edamame, or sliced mushrooms. Peanut sesame ramen offers a nutty and savory flavor profile that makes it a delicious and satisfying variation of the classic ramen dish.

Taiwanese Beef Noodle Soup

Ingredients:

For the Beef Broth:

    2 pounds beef shank or brisket, cut into chunks
    1 large onion, peeled and sliced
    4 cloves garlic, minced
    1 piece of ginger (about 2 inches), sliced
    1/2 cup soy sauce
    1/4 cup rice wine or Shaoxing wine
    2 tablespoons rock sugar or brown sugar
    1 cinnamon stick
    2 star anise
    3-4 dried red chili peppers (optional, for heat)
    8 cups water

For the Noodles and Toppings:

    Chinese wheat noodles or ramen noodles
    Bok choy, baby bok choy, or Shanghai bok choy, washed and trimmed
    Green onions, sliced
    Fresh cilantro leaves
    Red chili oil or chili sauce (optional, for added heat)

Instructions:

For the Beef Broth:

    In a large pot, bring water to a boil. Add the beef chunks and boil for 5 minutes. Discard the water and rinse the beef under cold water to remove impurities.
    In the same pot, add sliced onion, minced garlic, sliced ginger, soy sauce, rice wine, rock sugar or brown sugar, cinnamon stick, star anise, dried red chili peppers (if using), and 8 cups of water.
    Bring the mixture to a boil, then reduce the heat to simmer. Cover and let it simmer for at least 1.5 to 2 hours, or until the beef is tender and flavorful.
    Skim off any impurities that rise to the surface during the simmering process.
    Once the beef is tender, remove it from the broth and slice it into thin pieces.

For the Noodles and Toppings:

Cook the Chinese wheat noodles or ramen noodles according to the package instructions. Drain and set aside.

In a separate pot, blanch the bok choy in hot water for about 1-2 minutes until just tender. Remove and set aside.

Assemble Taiwanese Beef Noodle Soup:

- Divide the cooked noodles among serving bowls.
- Place slices of the cooked beef on top of the noodles.
- Add bok choy and ladle the hot beef broth over the noodles.
- Garnish with sliced green onions and fresh cilantro leaves.
- If you like it spicy, add a drizzle of red chili oil or your favorite chili sauce.
- Serve immediately and enjoy your authentic Taiwanese Beef Noodle Soup!

Feel free to customize the recipe based on your preferences. Taiwanese Beef Noodle Soup is known for its rich and aromatic broth, tender beef, and delicious noodles, making it a comforting and satisfying meal.

Tomato Basil Ramen

Ingredients:

- 2 packs of ramen noodles (discard the seasoning packets or use them if you prefer)
- 1 tablespoon olive oil
- 1 onion, finely chopped
- 3 cloves garlic, minced
- 1 can (14 oz) diced tomatoes
- 1 can (14 oz) crushed tomatoes
- 4 cups vegetable or chicken broth
- 1 teaspoon dried basil (or use fresh basil if available)
- Salt and pepper to taste
- Optional toppings: fresh basil leaves, grated Parmesan cheese, red pepper flakes

Instructions:

Cook the ramen noodles according to the package instructions. Drain and set aside.
In a large pot, heat the olive oil over medium heat. Add the chopped onion and sauté until softened and translucent.
Add the minced garlic and sauté for an additional 1-2 minutes until fragrant.
Pour in the diced tomatoes and crushed tomatoes with their juices. Stir well to combine.
Add the vegetable or chicken broth to the pot. Bring the mixture to a simmer and let it cook for about 10-15 minutes to allow the flavors to meld.
Stir in the dried basil and season the soup with salt and pepper to taste.
Once the soup has simmered and the flavors have developed, add the cooked ramen noodles to the pot. Stir to combine and heat through.
Serve the Tomato Basil Ramen hot, garnished with fresh basil leaves, grated Parmesan cheese, and a sprinkle of red pepper flakes if you like.

Feel free to customize this recipe to your liking, adding other vegetables or protein sources such as tofu or shredded chicken. Enjoy your delicious and comforting Tomato Basil Ramen!

Shrimp and Coconut Ramen

Ingredients:

- 2 packs of ramen noodles
- 1 tablespoon vegetable oil
- 1 onion, finely chopped
- 3 cloves garlic, minced
- 1 tablespoon ginger, grated
- 1 pound (450g) shrimp, peeled and deveined
- 1 can (14 oz) coconut milk
- 4 cups chicken or vegetable broth
- 2 tablespoons soy sauce
- 1 tablespoon fish sauce
- 1 tablespoon brown sugar
- Juice of 1 lime
- Salt and pepper to taste
- Optional toppings: chopped green onions, cilantro, lime wedges, red chili flakes

Instructions:

Cook the ramen noodles according to the package instructions. Drain and set aside.

In a large pot, heat the vegetable oil over medium heat. Add the chopped onion and sauté until softened.

Add the minced garlic and grated ginger to the pot. Sauté for an additional 1-2 minutes until fragrant.

Add the shrimp to the pot and cook until they turn pink and opaque, about 2-3 minutes.

Pour in the coconut milk and chicken or vegetable broth. Stir well to combine.

Add soy sauce, fish sauce, brown sugar, and lime juice to the pot. Season with salt and pepper to taste.

Let the soup simmer for about 5-7 minutes to allow the flavors to meld and the shrimp to cook through.

Once the soup is ready, divide the cooked ramen noodles among serving bowls and ladle the shrimp and coconut broth over them.

Garnish with chopped green onions, cilantro, and a lime wedge. If you like a bit of heat, sprinkle with red chili flakes.

Serve immediately and enjoy your Shrimp and Coconut Ramen!

Feel free to customize the recipe by adding vegetables like spinach, bok choy, or mushrooms for added flavor and nutrition.

Chicken Katsu Ramen

Ingredients:

For Chicken Katsu:

- 2 boneless, skinless chicken breasts
- Salt and pepper, to taste
- 1/2 cup all-purpose flour
- 2 large eggs, beaten
- 1 cup panko breadcrumbs
- Vegetable oil for frying

For Ramen:

- 2 packs of ramen noodles
- 1 tablespoon vegetable oil
- 1 onion, thinly sliced
- 3 cloves garlic, minced
- 1 tablespoon ginger, grated
- 4 cups chicken broth
- 2 tablespoons soy sauce
- 1 tablespoon mirin (Japanese sweet rice wine)
- 1 tablespoon sesame oil

Toppings:

- Sliced green onions
- Nori (seaweed) strips
- Sesame seeds
- Thinly sliced cabbage or spinach (optional)

Instructions:

Chicken Katsu:

Preheat the oven to 350°F (180°C).

Season the chicken breasts with salt and pepper.
Dredge each chicken breast in flour, dip into beaten eggs, and coat with panko breadcrumbs, pressing the breadcrumbs onto the chicken to adhere.
Heat vegetable oil in a large skillet over medium-high heat. Fry the chicken breasts until golden brown and cooked through, about 4-5 minutes per side.
Place the cooked chicken on a baking sheet and bake in the preheated oven for an additional 10 minutes to ensure it's cooked through.
Once baked, let the chicken rest for a few minutes, then slice into strips.

Ramen:

Cook the ramen noodles according to the package instructions. Drain and set aside.
In a large pot, heat vegetable oil over medium heat. Add sliced onions, minced garlic, and grated ginger. Sauté until the onions are tender.
Pour in the chicken broth and bring to a simmer. Add soy sauce, mirin, and sesame oil. Adjust the seasoning to taste.
Assemble the ramen bowls by placing a portion of cooked noodles into each bowl. Ladle the hot broth over the noodles.
Top the ramen with slices of chicken katsu, sliced green onions, nori strips, sesame seeds, and any additional toppings you prefer.
Serve the Chicken Katsu Ramen hot and enjoy!

Feel free to customize the recipe by adding vegetables or adjusting the seasonings to suit your taste.

Tantanmen

Ingredients:

For the Tantanmen Sauce:

- 2 tablespoons sesame paste (or tahini)
- 2 tablespoons soy sauce
- 1 tablespoon miso paste
- 1 tablespoon chili oil (adjust to taste for spice level)
- 1 tablespoon sugar
- 2 cloves garlic, minced
- 1 teaspoon grated ginger
- 1 cup chicken or vegetable broth

For the Ramen:

- 2 packs of ramen noodles
- 1 tablespoon vegetable oil
- 1 onion, finely chopped
- 1/2 pound (225g) ground pork or chicken
- 2 cups bok choy or spinach, chopped
- 4 cups chicken or vegetable broth
- Salt to taste
- Chopped green onions and sesame seeds for garnish

Instructions:

Tantanmen Sauce:

In a bowl, whisk together sesame paste, soy sauce, miso paste, chili oil, sugar, minced garlic, and grated ginger until well combined.
Gradually add chicken or vegetable broth to the mixture, stirring continuously until you achieve a smooth and creamy consistency. Set aside.

Ramen:

Cook the ramen noodles according to the package instructions. Drain and set aside.

In a large pot, heat vegetable oil over medium heat. Add chopped onions and sauté until they become translucent.

Add ground pork or chicken to the pot and cook until browned.

Pour in the chicken or vegetable broth and bring to a simmer. Season with salt to taste.

Add the prepared Tantanmen sauce to the broth and stir well to combine. Simmer for an additional 5-7 minutes.

In the last couple of minutes, add chopped bok choy or spinach to the pot and cook until just wilted.

Divide the cooked ramen noodles among serving bowls and ladle the Tantanmen broth over them.

Garnish with chopped green onions and sesame seeds.

Serve the Tantanmen hot and enjoy your flavorful and spicy Japanese-Chinese noodle dish!

Feel free to customize the recipe by adjusting the spice level, adding other vegetables, or incorporating your favorite protein sources.

Tempura Udon

Ingredients:

For the Tempura:

- Assorted vegetables (e.g., sweet potato, zucchini, bell pepper, and/or broccoli), sliced into bite-sized pieces
- Shrimp, peeled and deveined
- 1 cup all-purpose flour
- 1 cup ice-cold water
- Ice cubes
- Vegetable oil for frying
- Salt and pepper to taste

For the Udon Broth:

- 4 cups dashi (Japanese soup stock)
- 1/4 cup soy sauce
- 2 tablespoons mirin
- 1 tablespoon sake
- 1 tablespoon sugar
- Salt to taste

For the Udon Noodles:

- 2 packs of pre-cooked udon noodles

Toppings:

- Green onions, finely chopped
- Nori (seaweed) strips
- Shichimi togarashi (Japanese seven-spice blend)

Instructions:

Tempura:

> In a mixing bowl, combine flour and ice-cold water. Stir gently until just combined (the batter should be slightly lumpy). Add ice cubes to keep the batter cold.

Heat vegetable oil in a deep fryer or a large pot to 350°F (175°C).
Dip the sliced vegetables and shrimp into the tempura batter, allowing excess batter to drip off.
Carefully place the coated vegetables and shrimp into the hot oil and fry until golden brown and crispy. Work in batches to avoid overcrowding the fryer.
Remove the tempura from the oil and place on a paper towel-lined plate. Season with salt and pepper.

Udon Broth:

In a separate pot, combine dashi, soy sauce, mirin, sake, and sugar. Bring the mixture to a simmer over medium heat.
Adjust the seasoning with salt to taste.

Udon Noodles:

Cook the udon noodles according to the package instructions. Drain and set aside.
Divide the cooked udon noodles among serving bowls.

Assembling Tempura Udon:

Pour the hot udon broth over the noodles in each bowl.
Arrange the tempura (vegetables and shrimp) on top of the noodles and broth.
Garnish with finely chopped green onions, nori strips, and a sprinkle of shichimi togarashi for added spice.
Serve the Tempura Udon hot and enjoy the delightful combination of crispy tempura and savory udon in a flavorful broth.

Feel free to customize the recipe by adding additional toppings such as grated daikon radish or tempura dipping sauce on the side.